The Writer's Express
Grades 6-8

by Rebekah Woodie and Judy Light Ayyildiz

illustrated by Elizabeth Adams

cover by Jeff Van Kanegan

Publisher
Instructional Fair • TS Denison
Grand Rapids, Michigan 49544

ISBN: 1-56822-863-5
The Writer's Express Grades 6-8
Copyright © 1999 by Ideal • Instructional Fair
a division of Tribune Education
2400 Turner Avenue NW
Grand Rapids, Michigan 49544

TABLE OF CONTENTS

Narrative Writing 1
Double Trouble 2
This Week's Story 3
Sign Language 4
Your Dream Vacation 5
The Point That Determines the End 6
Scarred for Life 8
A Flashback in Time 9
Symbolic Ideas 11
Understanding Allegory 12
Changing Your Point of View 13
Finding What You Have Lost 14
Stepping Away from Yourself 15

Descriptive Writing 17
A Shell Full of Memories 18
What Would You Miss? 19
Self-Defense 20
That Same Familiar Sound 21
Meeting Your Dream Person 22
Imagine This 23
First View 24
Second View 25
Express Yourself 26
A Matter of Fact 27
Do Not Take an Everyday Noun for Granted 28
Your Moods as Similes 29
Sounds Like Something I Know 30
Your Hands Can Do It 31
Excuse Me While I Exaggerate My Appreciation 32
You Just Have to Want This Product! 33
The Urge to Travel 35

Writing Poetry 37
Unfolding Poems 38
Lines That Stop in the Middle 40
Talking Objects 41
The Most Exciting Holiday of the Year 42
You Get Your Fingers in Everything! 44
Images of Strangers 45
Naming the Sounds of the Scene 47
Permission to Experience the Subject 49
Formula Poem 51
Acrostic Poems Are Worth a Fortune 53
Look at the Shape Things Are In 54
A Lovely Lyric 55
Couplets Rhyme at Thanksgiving Time 56
For You a Haiku, Valentine 57
A Select Free Verse 59

Island Poem 60
Category Poem 62
Short and Smart Things to Say in Verse 63
A Long-Lasting Verse 65
Poems of Common Sense and Nonsense 66

Writing Drama 67
Get Ready, Get Set, Go On with the Show 68
Important Properties 69
Wearing the Right Costume 71
Write the Right Name and You Won't Go Wrong 72
The Imaginary Time Machine 74
Finding a Solution 75
Talking It Over with Yourself 77
In the Spotlight 79
A Spring Holiday Creation of Mime 81

Speech Writing 82
Opposites Attract 83
Ironically Speaking 85
Explaining the Process 86
Persuading Others to Mind Their Manners 87
An Address with a Symbol 89
Never Speechless 91

Expository Writing 93
You Should Read This Book 94
Two Thumbs Up! 96
Passing Notes 97
To Say Something Nice 98
A Different Kind of Friend 99
The Reporter's "Five and One" 100
Your Mind's Eye 102
Things to Keep in Your Journal 103
What Is Fun and What Is Not! 104
Do You Measure Up? 106
What's in a Name? 107
Exploring Connections and Contrasts 108
Wishing Words 110
May I Introduce Myself? 111
Video Game Fever 113

Research Writing 114
Little-Known Facts 115
Investigating an Endangered Species on the Internet 116
Your Hometown Climate, "Weather" You Like It or Not 118
What If It Did Not Happen That Way? 119
Research and Rewrite It in Your Own Words 120
Selecting the Best 121

How to Use the Writer's Express

The activities in this book streamline the teaching of writing. With these precise, step-by-step instructions, teachers and students can easily follow through each lesson. Although these writing lessons are planned in simple-to-follow formats, each was designed to be intriguing while communicating a fundamental writing skill.

The book is composed of seven sections of writing activities for the following literary genres.

Narrative Writing (short scenes and stories)
Descriptive Writing (writing descriptive paragraphs)
Writing Poetry (20 different types of poems)
Writing Drama (script writing and theater craft)
Speech Writing (public speech making)
Expository Writing (essay writing skills)
Research Writing (basic research techniques)

The authors have many years experience in teaching writing. For this reason, teachers who use this book can be assured that its methodology is based on actual classroom experience. It is not necessary to consume valuable planning time developing lesson plans. Each section employs critical thinking as a primary method to build writing skills. To clarify the writing process for students, each section applies basic brainstorming, prewriting, and then rewriting strategies. Using a personalized approach, every lesson also teaches the essential elements for the particular literary genre included in this book. Student confidence in writing skills has always had a direct correlation to the ability to write well. Each lesson has been designed so that students can be successful, therefore, enabling them to boost their self-confidence and natural creative ability.

The activities in *The Writer's Express* are loaded with all the writing techniques and skills required for the sixth- through eighth-grade. The exercises range from easy to difficult. You will be able to assess quickly the difficulty level for your students. Each activity stands alone; however, a glance at any section reveals how lessons can be combined or sequenced according to your students' needs.

Every lesson is ready-made for the classroom. To prepare for teaching an activity, choose any of the one- or two-page lessons from the particular genre you want to study. Simply duplicate the activity and distribute it to your class. All the activities lend themselves to independent student work.

Although most of the student writing is completed on the activity sheet, some activities will require students to use their own notebook paper. The authors suggest that students maintain individual writing folders or journals. Their ideas and rough drafts can be kept for future writing assignments. Using these procedures, students can monitor their own progress. You, too, can access their folders or journals as valuable tools for an alternative assessment.

Whether you make this book a classroom supplement or your basic writing text, you can depend on its quality and variety. This book's easy-to-follow format was created specifically to enable any teacher or home schooler to incorporate the writing assignments across the curriculum.

All aboard *The Writer's Express!*

Section 1

Narrative Writing

DOUBLE TROUBLE

Mom went out for her walk early in the morning. Keith and Rachel were not up yet; today was a vacation day from school. As soon as the door squeaked closed, Rachel woke up ready to start her day. She went downstairs and was about to pour the milk over her cereal when her cats came running through the kitchen. They jostled her feet that tilted her hands that held the gallon of milk that was always too heavy for her eight-year-old arms. Milk spilled everywhere.

What could she do? Then she noticed that her brother was awake and playing a video game in his room. Through the window, she saw Mom in the driveway, just about to come to the porch from her walk. What could she do? Take the rap for the spilt milk? NO WAY! Much better to get her big brother into trouble. So she zoomed upstairs, jumped into bed, covered up her head, and began to snore. What happened next? You guessed it — "Keith! Come in here and clean up this milk!"

It seems so much easier to get someone else in trouble rather than to take the punishment yourself! Has a similar scene happened to you?

Imagine a story about one time when you got someone into trouble on purpose. What happened? Were you ever found out? Did he or she do anything for revenge? Or were you just getting that person back for something he or she had done to you earlier? Write the story from your point of view. You may use other paper to complete your story.

_____

_____

_____

_____

_____

_____

After you have completed your side of the story, write the story from the other person's point of view.

THIS WEEK'S STORY

A short story has a beginning, middle, and end. Every story creates a problem to solve. The conflict may include one or more characters who struggle with the problem. Near the end of the story, something happens which determines how the story ends. This is the climax, or the *epiphany*, of the story.

CHARACTER: The character in this story will be you.

CONFLICT: Think of an event that caused you a problem. It can be small or large. For example, your mom's car got stuck on the way to soccer practice or you watched television too long and forgot to do your homework.

BEGINNING: Write how and where this event began. Write it as though you are telling the story to a friend. Include details that describe the sights, sounds, and smells in this scene. There should be action words (verbs) that show the conflict. Do not hesitate to invent details to make the scene more exciting.

MIDDLE: Use descriptions of things you see, hear, touch, taste, and smell while the event is happening. Use conversation. The dialogue does not have to be exactly what was said, but it should sound realistic. Add action as you struggle to solve your problem. Show what you are doing. The solution may not come easily, and you must show the problem with your descriptive details and action words. Do not solve the conflict yet. Invent anything that makes the story more interesting. Your story does not have to be true, although it can be true. It is your choice.

CLIMAX: At this point, some action or event happens that determines how your story ends. You may solve your problem, or you may not. Do not, however, make the climax too simple, such as "and then I woke up." An unexpected climax is best.

END: The ending is not as big as the middle, but it can have some dialogue. Your primary goal in the ending is to show what happens as the scene's action closes. You can have a happy or an unhappy ending, depending on the events at the climax. Do not end your story by explaining its meaning.

On another sheet of paper write a story which includes each of the above parts.

SIGN LANGUAGE

You are in a foreign country. You have written and addressed a letter to a friend back in the United States. On the street where your hotel is located, you find a post office. You do not speak the language of this country, but you want to mail this letter. Using only sign language, facial expressions, and body language, analyze the steps you must take to mail your letter. Read the following questions silently and decide how you would react to each situation.

1. By observing other patrons and the post office personnel, how will you determine which window, station, or desk sells stamps?
2. When you have the correct window and it is your turn for service, what kind of facial expressions can you use to show the post office employee a friendly greeting?
3. Using sign language, how will you show the officer where you want to send your letter?
4. When he or she speaks to you, what can you do to indicate that you do not speak his or her language?
5. How will you buy your stamp?
6. How will you indicate, "Thank you"?

Write a scene that shows your mailing a letter in a foreign country. You can use only sign language, body movements, and facial expressions. Follow the instructions below.

1. Begin your story as you enter the post office with the letter in your hand.
2. Write your story from the third person point of view as in the following example.
   Karen pulled on the heavy latch to open the glass door. In her left hand, she held the letter to her brother Kevin. Karen imagined how thrilled Kevin would be to receive mail from Paris, France.
3. Include details which describe the place. What do you and other people there look like? What is everyone doing?
4. Include descriptions of sounds you hear (doors opening and closing, feet moving, paper rustling).
5. Include what you are feeling and thinking as the action happens. Do not be concerned that you may have never had such an experience. You are creating an imaginary scene.

Read your story to the class. How is your narrative different from the others?

YOUR DREAM VACATION

The breeze blew softly over my suntanned body as I lay on the dark beach of Maui. A wisp of a cloud floated at the horizon, and seagulls plunged into the waves for fish. The radio played at my side as I sipped on a frosty soft drink. I dug my toes into the warm sand and brushed a few beads of sweat off my forehead. I had nowhere to go, nothing to do, but lie in the sun and listen to the calm ocean waves.

Does this narrative sound like a dream vacation? What is your dream vacation? Where would you go? What would you do? Could you describe your dream vacation so that the reader is able to see and experience the vacation along with you? What do you see? Hear? Smell? Taste? Touch? Give details and describe it as though you were actually there today!

_____

_____

_____

_____

_____

_____

_____

_____

_____

_____

_____

_____

_____

_____

_____

_____

THE POINT THAT DETERMINES THE END

A story is about one or more characters involved in a conflict. One type of problem characters experience is internal conflict.

Consider this character's problem: Hillary's internal conflict is a moral issue. Should she remain silent and let her mom deal with the embarrassment and frustration of why her famous cake she baked for the big party turned out to be a dismal failure? Or should she be truthful and relieve her mom's confusion and allow her to save face as a cook? The conflict here is that when Hillary tells her that *she* broke a rule about opening the oven door on a baking cake, she will have to face Mom's anger.

Obviously, this family story has a beginning (Mom planning the party and preparing the cake), a middle (the part where Hillary comes to the kitchen and opens the oven door), and an end. The end will depend on the decision Hillary makes to resolve her internal conflict.

In every story, there is one point that determines the end. It is called the *climax*. At the climax of the example story, Hillary will either tell the truth or hide the truth. The two choices will provide two different endings.

Think of a situation that has happened in your family. This situation must be one in which the main character has an internal conflict. After you have chosen the situation you want to use, consider the nature of the problem. What was the beginning of it? The middle?

Situation with an internal conflict _____

Main character _____

What did your main character do to cause this internal conflict? _____

_____

_____

_____

_____

Beginning _____

_____

_____

Middle_____

_____

_____

Write what happens at the climax of your story. Remember that the climax is the point in the story at which some decision is made that determines the end. It will bring your story to a conclusion, whether it is a happy or a sad ending. Be exact in your details.

Climax_____

_____

_____

End _____

_____

_____

Explain how your story might have ended if another decision had been made at the climax.

_____

_____

_____

_____

_____

_____

_____

_____

_____

_____

_____

_____

_____

SCARRED FOR LIFE

A *memoir* is a true story. It can be about an outstanding person, or it can focus on a significant event that brought about personal or social change. You can also write a memoir about something meaningful that has happened in your life.

Think about a time in your life when one of your possessions was damaged or when you got a scar on your body. Choose either type of problem and write your memoir.

Questions to think about as you write your memoir.

1. What is the scar or damaged object? Describe how it looks today. Where is it?
2. What happened just before the event took place?
3. Did you expect this event to happen? Why?
4. For what reason did the damage or scar happen?
5. What important people or other objects were part of the event?
6. What were the details and the actions?
7. How did you react or cope with the problem?
8. How did you overcome the problem?
9. What did you learn?
10. What has changed as a result of this problem?

When you have completed the first draft on a separate sheet of paper, read it aloud.

Write another draft. Delete unnecessary information. Use any details you may have forgotten but are now able to remember.

A Flashback in Time

A *flashback* is a term used to define a point in a story where the narrative jumps back to previous action. The events of the plot are not always in chronological order. Sometimes it is more interesting for the story to begin in the middle or at the end, and then use flashbacks to earlier action. This device allows the reader to discover information gradually about events and characters.

Select one of your favorite family stories. It should involve you and a family member.

Write the main characters' names and the general idea of the story.

_____   _____

Example: Cousin JoAnn graduating from high school with her daughter, Kelly

Example: The applause filled Kelly's ears as if she had been elevated half a mile above Niagara Falls. She was bouncing on the proud beating of her heart. JoAnn, her mom, was at the podium on the stage, appreciatively nodding her head in her quiet way. The reception of Mom's valedictorian speech was like an exclamation point to Kelly's realization of an old cliché—it is never too late to follow your dreams.

Write the last scene of your family story. This scene should include the place where it happens, your main character and those characters involved in the action, and the action ending the story. Include any sensory details of sight, sound, taste, touch, and smell for description.

_____

_____

_____

_____

_____

_____

_____

It could be very intriguing if you began your family story with the ending. Your readers will be curious as to the events that led up to the last scene. If a story begins at the very end, everything else will be a flashback.

Read a flashback written for the example story.

"I'll be so embarrassed!" Kelly screamed before running out of the house. The screen door slammed behind her. She caught hold of the black chain that held the porch swing. The front yard and the quiet street beyond were a watery blur. She hopped off the low porch. The grass was cool on her bare feet. She jammed her hands into the pockets of her cut-off jeans and ambled over to sit under the old willow tree. "Nobody goes to school with their mother!" she thought. She could just picture herself next month walking into the school through the heavy double doors with Mom. So what if JoAnn Jones had had to drop out of high school to get married. So what if now that the kids were getting grown she had a chance to become a registered nurse. "This is my senior year," Kelly mumbled. She sucked a bead of tear into her lips. It would just never work, that's all.

Reread the ending of your story, and write a flashback. Select one of the events that leads up to the end. Use details and action. Create several lines of dialogue between characters. Make the flashback longer than the ending you wrote.

_____

_____

_____

_____

_____

_____

_____

_____

_____

_____

_____

Symbolic Ideas

In 1912 *Titanic*, the largest passenger ship ever built, scraped an iceberg and sank while crossing the Atlantic Ocean from the British Isles. Those in charge made careless and fatal mistakes because people believed *Titanic* could not sink. Only a day or two away from New York City's safe harbor, 1,522 passengers and crew lost their lives. The word, *titanic*, remains today as a symbol for something either gigantic or disastrous or both. A *symbol* is a person, place, or object that represents a larger idea.

Below is a list of words that have become symbolic through the years. The information associated with them includes impressive stories and important lessons. Write a symbolic idea beside at least four of the following words.

A clown _____   The telephone _____

The Mississippi River_____   The *Hindenburg* _____

Thomas Edison _____   A shovel _____

The Boston Tea Party _____   Venus _____

The Little Red Hen _____   The wheel_____

Choose an event from your life. For example, if you have experienced playing a significant part in a successful holiday pageant, this event would represent a huge success in your life. A good symbol for this successful event would be a "dinosaur."

Write the event you have chosen to symbolize. Beside it, write what the event represents in your life. In the last blank, write a symbol for this experience.

Event _____What it represents _____Symbol _____

Write a story about your event. Create your story so that the word and the symbolism attached to it are the central idea of your narrative.

UNDERSTANDING ALLEGORY

An *allegory* is a story that is full of symbolic ideas. A *symbol* is the use of one thing to represent a larger idea. In a fairy tale allegory, such as *Little Red Riding Hood,* the grandmother represents the home, Riding Hood represents innocence going out into the world, and the wolf represents evil in the form of greed, violence, and deception. The woodsman represents the rescuers who overcome evil and put the world back in proper order. An allegory also teaches a lesson while it entertains. The lesson taught in *Little Red Riding Hood* is that good overcomes evil.

Choose your favorite traditional fairy tale from the many you know, such as *Beauty and the Beast, Hansel and Gretel, Snow White, Cinderella, Jack and the Bean Stalk,* or any other fairy tale.

1. Write out the basic story of the fairy tale you have chosen. Include all the characters, settings, and actions.

2. After you write your fairy tale, list its characters, settings, and actions. Then write what ideas these characters, settings, and actions symbolize.

For example:
　　　　Characters
The wolf represents greed and violence.
　　　　Settings
The forest represents the world.
　　　　Actions
The wolf disguised as grandmother represents deception.

These characters, settings, and actions and their representations make an allegory.

3. Create *modern* characters, settings, and actions to replace the traditional characters, settings, and actions from the fairy tale you selected. Replace each item on your list with a character, place, or action that matches the original item.
　　For example: Replace the wolf with a rat.
　　　　　　　　Replace the forest with an alley.
　　　　　　　　Replace the deceptive wolf with the rat handing out drugs as candy.
　　　　　　　　Replace Little Red Riding Hood with a student.

4. Write a modern allegory based on the replacements in your list. You should not explain the symbols that the characters, places, and actions represent. These ideas should be *shown* in your story.

CHANGING YOUR POINT OF VIEW

A basic element of a narrative, or story, is the point from which the action is viewed. The following narrative is told from the eyes (the view) of a narrator who can see everything that is happening. This point of view is a third person narrator.

Read this story as an example of a third person narrator.

Number 10, Billy Barker, bundled from head to toe in red and white wool and leather, dashes to the rear of the bobsled. He pushes off and jumps aboard with the three other members of his team. They whiz around the long, icy slope. The captain steers the front axle with a rope. The high walls of the path curve like the hump of a rainbow. Soon, the bobsledders are zinging swift as a rocket, going almost one hundred miles an hour. One more skidding curve, and Billy sights the straightaway. The roar of the steel runners fills his whole body as he crosses the finish line. Billy thinks: "Finally, I am a winner!"

The point of view of the example narrative shows a third person narrator who can see every detail. In this case, the third person narrator also knows the thoughts of one of the characters.

Stories can also be told from a first person point of view. This narrator can be a minor character such as one in a crowd in the story, this narrator can be the most important person in the scene, or this narrator does not have to be in the story at all. With a first person narrator, the story is limited to what this person can experience, think, or feel. The first person narrator can see through his or her eyes only. The first person narrator cannot know what others are thinking and feeling.

Rewrite the example above, keeping the details the same. But make one change. Change the viewpoint from the third person to first person.

_____

_____

_____

_____

_____

_____

_____

Name _____

FINDING WHAT YOU HAVE LOST

As you grow older, you are likely to change houses, clubs, friends, and activities. Perhaps sometimes you think of certain persons, places, or objects you used to be with quite often. You miss things of the past, but you can never have them back as they used to be.

Writing a letter to something or someone from the past is an excellent way to help you feel better about loss. It is not even necessary to send these letters to achieve this purpose.

Choose a subject—a person, place, or object—from your past that you still miss today. Write a letter to this subject.

Begin your letter by briefly telling about yourself today.

Next, write about what causes you to remember your subject.

Include actions and sensory details (sight, sound, taste, touch, and smell) to describe activities you shared with your subject.

In closing, explain why this memory is so important to you.

Read the example below.

> *Dear Seth,*
>
> *It has been a long time since we have seen each other. I have lived in Gordonville now for three years, and I go to William Clark Middle School. My favorite class is art. We do exciting projects. The other day when we were given the new activity of clay sculptures, I laughed out loud recalling one of my adventures with you. I was remembering the day we tried to make clay from the dirt in the puddle of my driveway and then put our "sculptures" in my mom's oven to bake. I'm not sure whether Mom ever got all of that mess out of the oven, but we have a new oven now! Even though you and I are too old to make sculptures out of driveway mud, I'll never forget the fun we had together.*
>
> *So long,*
> *Ben*

Stepping Away from Yourself

Choose an activity you do daily or weekly that involves your walking from one place to another. Perhaps you step out to the grocery store, walk the dog, go down the street to a friend's house, or walk to a mall for shopping.

1. Your choice:_____

     _____

2. Briefly describe what you wear._____

     _____

3. Describe two details of the weather.

     _____

4. Name two specific things you might see or encounter as you walk. Explain them and incorporate adjectives and action verbs into the explanation.

     _____

     _____

5. What are you thinking as you have your encounters along the way?

     _____

     _____

     _____

6. Write a narrative paragraph describing yourself as you go on this walk. Write the narrative from your point of view. (Use the "I" pronoun.)

_____

_____

_____

_____

_____

_____

_____

7. When you have finished writing, reread your narrative. Read it as though you have stepped outside yourself and have become another person reading about yourself. During this reading, imagine that you are watching yourself take this walk, having these encounters, thoughts, and feelings. If you were someone else, you would take this walk and have slightly different encounters. Maybe you would see the weather from a different view. Your thoughts and feelings may not be the same either.

8. Rewrite your narrative. This time write the paragraph from a third person viewpoint as though someone else were describing you and your walk. When you finish, compare your two points of view. How are they different?

_____

_____

_____

_____

_____

_____

_____

_____

_____

_____

_____

_____

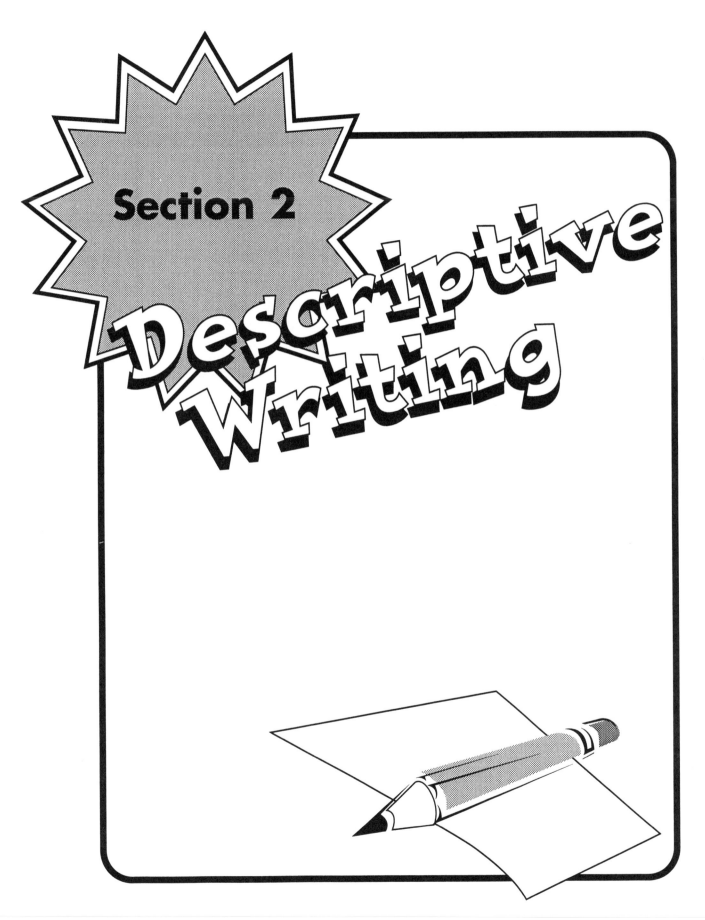

Section 2

Descriptive Writing

A Shell Full of Memories

A fun adventure at the beach is a hunt for the many different sizes, colors, and shapes of the shells that once were homes for various sea creatures. Washed up onto the shore, they are delightful treasures to find. Each empty shell holds a silent memory that could be described in a journal entry. Like a shell, you, too, have changed. Memories of the particular stages of your life are different from the life that you are experiencing today.

Imagine being at least several years younger than you are now. Perhaps you remember when you were a small child or in the first grades of elementary school. Choose a year in your life. What events, people, objects, and places were the most important to you in that year? What was your greatest disappointment or accomplishment of that year?

Select one scene of the year you chose that shows either a disappointment or an accomplishment, and write it on the line below.

_____

Write a journal entry you might have made on that particular day. Begin your entry with a month, a day, and the year. If you do not remember exactly, write what you remember them to be. *Example: December, Friday, 1996.*

Next, describe the scene: where you were, the sounds, the smells, and how it looked. Tell what happened. Explain why this event was either disappointing or successful.
For example: December, Friday, 1996. I was in the second grade at Carver School. When the teacher said on Thursday to write a holiday poem, my classmates complained, but I was excited. Soon after I stood up and began reading my 25 rhyming lines, the scooting of desks and feet, and the rattling of papers stopped. Everybody clapped and said my poem was the best. I didn't know I could do anything special. I thought everyone could just automatically write a poem. I learned I had a natural gift for putting words together, and I have continued always to write poems.

When you have finished your journal entry, read it aloud to the class.

Name _____

WHAT WOULD YOU MISS?

You wake up on any normal morning and rub the sleep out of your eyes. Everything is the same . . . right? Then you look out of the window. Wait a minute! Where are the cars? Why are there horse and buggies on the dirt streets? You have been magically transferred back to an earlier time—all the way back to your great-grandparents' days in the early twentieth century. The day passes as you wander through the town of your great-grandparents' youth. What is not in your great-grandparents' world that you take for granted in your world? What do you like better in your great-grandparents' world? What things are different? What things are the same?

Write a descriptive paragraph about a part of your day in your great-grandparents' world. Write the paragraph from your point of view. End the paragraph with an explanation of why you would rather stay in your great-grandparents' world or why you would rather come back to your world.

_____

_____

_____

_____

_____

_____

_____

_____

_____

_____

_____

_____

_____

_____

_____

_____

_____

_____

SELF-DEFENSE

At one time or another, most people have been accused of doing something they did not do. When that happens to you, it is likely you want to speak out and defend yourself. You may feel sad or angry.

Think of a time when you were unjustly accused. Make a list of what you remember about the incident. Include important details and specific descriptions. Who made the accusation? Why did they think you were the one at fault?

_____

_____

_____

_____

_____

_____

_____

_____

Write a letter to whoever made the false accusation. Explain your side of the story. Be clear and precise. Defend yourself by making several definite points. Get this false accusation "off your chest."

_____

_____

_____

_____

_____

_____

_____

_____

_____

Name _____

THAT SAME FAMILIAR SOUND

Imagine that you are alone in your house. A member of your family comes home. You cannot see him or her from where you are located in the house. Even though this person does not speak, chances are you recognize who the person is by the sound of his or her steps.

A person's footsteps may be prancing, hard, quick, or sluggish. We may also distinguish footsteps by the type of shoes the person is wearing.

Choose one member of your family. Answer the following questions to analyze his or her footsteps. Imagine that you are listening to him or her coming home.

1. What kind of shoes is this person wearing? _____

2. Describe this person's feet hitting the floor. _____

   _____

3. Describe the kind of steps he or she takes. _____

   _____

A *simile* is a comparison of one thing to another using *like* or *as*. The comparison is based on finding one or more features of both things that are similar. Write a simile that compares the sound of your family member's footsteps to something else, such as sounds in nature, noises around machines or animals, or any other type of sound. For example: *My mom's high heels make a clicking sound like a deer's hooves on rock.*

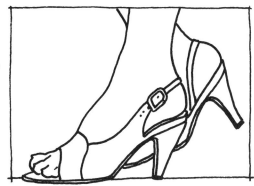

Write a paragraph that describes your family member's footsteps. Use your responses to the questions and your simile to get started.

Read your paragraph to your family. If they know right away whom you have described, you will know that you have written a very accurate description.

MEETING YOUR DREAM PERSON

Did you ever wonder how someone meets the person of his or her dreams? Have you ever thought about meeting such a person? Where would it happen? What would you say? What would he or she say? Most importantly, *who* is this person of your dreams? Some popular movie or television star, a sports champion, or someone you create?

Write a paragraph in the outline of the person below that describes meeting the person of your dreams. Be specific and save this paragraph in your diary or scrapbook. It will be exciting to see if your meeting with this dream person comes true!

IMAGINE THIS

What is happening in the above sketch? Where is this person? What does she have on her feet and in her hands?

List two things you see in the picture.
For example: mountains, snow

_____   _____

Write two adjectives that will tell more about the things you listed.
For example: steep mountains, feathery snow

_____   _____

List two actions you see in the picture.
For example: hurl, churn

_____   _____

Write a description about the drawing above. Include the six words you have listed above.
For example: She hurls herself down the steep mountain. Jabbing through clusters of feathery snow, she churns up the white powder beneath her feet.

_____

_____

_____

_____

_____

First View

When you visit an area where you have not been, you will notice the surrounding scenery, the buildings, the style of clothing, the methods of transportation, the way the people speak, and other things different from your hometown.

Imagine yourself in a town located in a foreign country. Think of a country, other than the United States, that either you have visited, read about, or seen on film.

Write the name of a town in a foreign country: _____

List of differences (sights, sounds, lifestyles) between this town and a town in the United States:

_____

_____

_____

_____

_____

_____

Write about your walking or riding through the streets of the town in the foreign country you selected. Use your list for ideas. Write from your personal point of view. Write about what you see and what you are thinking about as you encounter the environment. Include your feelings about being a foreigner in this strange environment. Since you are writing only what you see, hear, taste, touch, smell, and feel, you are writing in the first person point of view.

_____

_____

_____

_____

_____

_____

_____

_____

SECOND VIEW

Your hometown is a very familiar place. You know many things about it. By pretending to be a foreigner from another country, you can describe your hometown as though you are seeing it for the first time.

Imagine that a person your age from a foreign country came to your hometown to visit for the first time. List several things your foreigner would see, hear, smell, taste, and touch. Add any other details that would be strange to him or her.

_____

_____

_____

_____

_____

Write a description from a first person point of view as though you were a foreigner in your hometown. Write as though you are walking through the town. Use the ideas from your list to help you describe how you, as the foreigner, are seeing your hometown now.

_____

_____

_____

_____

_____

_____

When you are finished, read your description aloud. How did other students describe your hometown?

Name _____

EXPRESS YOURSELF

"Don't look a gift horse in the mouth." "The grass is always greener on the other side." "Nervous as a long-tailed cat in a room full of rocking chairs."

What could these expressions possibly mean? You may have heard or even used one of them. These expressions are old sayings or proverbs invented by people who made accurate observations about human nature.

"Don't look a gift horse in the mouth," came from a selling practice in horse trading. A horse's teeth reveal its age. Therefore, when buying a horse, the buyers always looked into the horse's mouth to judge whether or not the horse was a good buy. If, however, a person should give you a horse, it is impolite to look in its mouth. Knowing human nature, we understand that we should not determine the value of a gift while the giver is around.

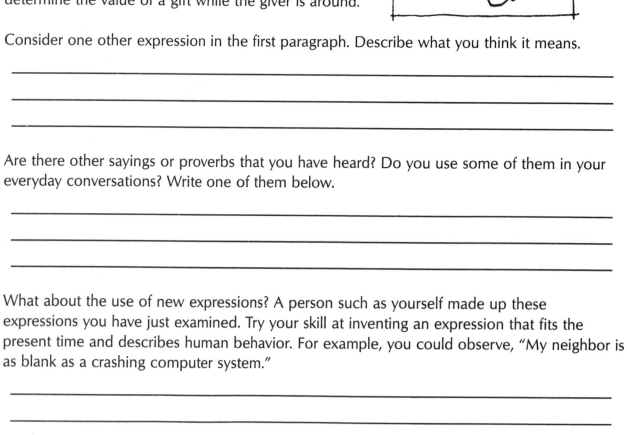

Consider one other expression in the first paragraph. Describe what you think it means.

_____

_____

_____

Are there other sayings or proverbs that you have heard? Do you use some of them in your everyday conversations? Write one of them below.

_____

_____

_____

What about the use of new expressions? A person such as yourself made up these expressions you have just examined. Try your skill at inventing an expression that fits the present time and describes human behavior. For example, you could observe, "My neighbor is as blank as a crashing computer system."

_____

_____

_____

A Matter of Fact

The following words do not create a detailed mental picture of an idea: *good, bad, ugly, horrible, wonderful, beautiful, lovely, awful.* These are only some of the many opinion words used daily. These opinion words, however, only give a general point of view about an idea. They do not create specific pictures.

On the other hand, words that convey facts are specific: *parched, torn, gully.* These words create a mental picture. The more specific words you use in your description, the more precise your images will be. You cannot create a specific image using opinion words.

Fill in the second column with specific words that describe the opinion word in the first column. In the third column, add adjectives or adverbs that further describe the image.

Opinion Word	Specific Words	More Detail
Examples: ugly	*a hillside torn open by erosion*	*parched, roughly, rude*
1. wonderful	_____	_____
2. awful	_____	_____
3. lovely	_____	_____

Choose one of your three images from the second column. On notebook paper, write a descriptive paragraph about the image you selected. Include specific words that make your description clear. Add details to make it precise.

For example: A parched hillside has been torn open by erosion. Even the fingers of the wind recoil at the touch of the rough hillside. Its once lush pastures and dense woods are now replaced by gullies and shaved bare dirt. The earth movers do their work for progress. The animals have no homes, and the people have no grass and trees.

Do Not Take an Everyday Noun for Granted

Nouns are names of persons, places, and things. While people depend on these everyday nouns, they give them no special thought. Do you take your everyday nouns for granted?

milk tub dog home air water sun

Describe the sound of a family member's voice. What is there about it that makes you feel loved? Place in quotation marks one of his or her most common sayings.

_____

_____

_____

Another everyday thing we take for granted is the smell of freshly cut grass. Describe this smell. Avoid nonspecific words that do not describe, like *sweet* or *tart.* Think of words that show how it smells like something else.
For example: pungent as sliced watermelon

_____

_____

Describe the place you like to be when it rains. Why? How does it make you feel?

_____

_____

_____

Select an everyday noun that you tend to take for granted. Use specific words to describe it. Use comparisons. Show what it looks like and how it sounds. If it has a smell or a taste, describe it.
For example: The silky touch of my grandmother's hand was like the wind's caress on my back.

_____

_____

_____

Your Moods as Similes

A simile uses the words *like* or *as* to compare one or more similar aspects of two different ideas—for example, "the bored student sat in the back of the classroom like a frog on a clump of mud." The simile "like a frog on a clump of mud" enhances the feeling of the bored student and makes a precise picture of the student in the reader's mind.

Words used to express emotions are abstract. For example, mood words, such as *happy, sad, depressed, joyous, empty, filled, cheerful, contented, angry, resentful,* or *sorrowful,* all give information. However, they do not create a precise picture in the reader's mind. By using a simile, you can make the expression of your mood exact—for example, "I'm contented as eight inches of fallen snow in orange-frosted moonlight." By combining the idea of contentment with the peaceful, heavy, quiet, beautiful snow under the light of the moon at night, the writer can clearly portray the mood to the reader.

Select one of the many moods you have experienced.

Mood: _____

Choose a place that brings a picture to your mind similar in feeling to the mood you have chosen.

Place: _____

Write the simile that expresses your chosen mood by comparing it with a description of your place.
For example: depressed as dried grass in a February thaw, nestled in the pasture, hoping for spring

_____

_____

_____

_____

SOUNDS LIKE SOMETHING I KNOW

Considering all of the objects that you own, which is your favorite? A teddy bear, a journal, a baseball glove, an old shirt, or a cap with the name of the best team in the world?

What activity or activities are associated with your favorite object? _____

_____

Describe the action involved with it. _____

_____

Whether quiet or loud, what are the sounds this object makes? What sounds are associated with it or what sounds often surround it?
For example: yelling, running of feet, scratching of a pencil, whacking of a bat

_____

Draw a large outline of the shape of your favorite object.

Onomatopoeia is a writing technique in which words sound like what they are.
For example, *growl*, *whine*, and *smack* are words whose sounds imitate their meanings.

Reread the ideas you wrote about your object. Think of two onomatopoetic words that can describe an action, activity, or sound associated with the object.

Inside the shape that you drew, write about your favorite object. Include your ideas and the two descriptive words that are onomatopoetic.

Name _____

YOUR HANDS CAN DO IT

Your hands are marvelous tools. They are designed to serve you in a variety of ways. Hands work independently or together. Fingers and palms move and shape to accommodate a hundred different needs every day.

Look at your hands and think of them as tools to serve you. For example, your hands could be like spades, power drivers, or cups. Verbs that describe the action of these three examples are "spades plunge and dig," "power drivers pound and slam," "cups hold and surround."

List two tasks your hands do daily for you. Beside each task on the list, write the name of a tool that your hands must mimic to do this task.

Task: Tool:
Example: wet my face with water   *Example: dippers*

1. _____   _____

2. _____   _____

Write one or two verbs that describe the action the hands perform when accomplishing these two tasks. Think of the tools the hand is mimicking and the actions they make.
For example: Task—wet my face with water. Tool—dippers. Verbs—toss, throw, splash

_____

_____

Write a description that compares your hands to tools. Include the verbs you chose to describe the action.

_____

_____

_____

_____

_____

_____

_____

_____

Excuse Me While I Exaggerate My Appreciation

Mother's Day and Father's Day allow you to express a friendly thank you to those special people. It is almost impossible to thank someone completely who has taken care of your needs for so many years. Do you ever wish you had the money and power to give your parents something really fantastic?

You can express your appreciation through words. An effective way to let someone know how much you care is to use overstatement or hyperbole. Letting your mother and father know that you notice their personal wishes and desires can make them feel great.

Think of either your mother or your father. Consider the kinds of things that parent really likes to do, your parent's hobbies or dreams. Has your parent talked about taking a particular trip, perhaps to an exotic place? Or would your parent relish having lots of time for reading, gardening, hunting, or painting? Or perhaps your parent would like to star in a play or sing at the Metropolitan Opera in New York City. Maybe Mom or Dad would just like to visit someone special.

Write a Mother's Day or Father's Day wish. Begin by explaining how you feel. Then describe the one special event you would arrange if you could make dreams come true. Use hyperbole to exaggerate what you would orchestrate if you were able. Be specific and include lots of description of this event.

_____

_____

_____

_____

_____

_____

_____

_____

You Just Have to Want This Product!

Think of some of the most popular consumer products on the market today. Why are some brands of toothpaste, tennis shoes, bean bag toys, cola, canned soup, fast foods, electronic pets, computer games, and types of music more successful than others?

Members of any certain group will naturally tend to buy products that are currently popular. But what makes a product generally desirable? When marketing a product, the professionals give prime consideration to WHAT purpose the product is going to serve, WHO is going to want to buy it, and WHY people are going to want it. Then the advertising is created to sell the product.

Among other things, successful advertising means devising slogans that say the most with the fewest words.

Invent a product that you would like to have for yourself, something you would use almost every day, something you would really enjoy. It should be one of your necessities, such as a food, a drink, a tool, a piece of clothing, an accessory, or a game. Perhaps you can think of another category for a new product you would buy if you could.

What would it be? _____

_____

What purpose is it going to serve? _____

_____

Who is going to want to buy it?_____

_____

Why are they going to want to buy it? _____

_____

In the space below, draw a picture of your new product. Label all important parts, noting size, its material, color, and any other detail.

Create a one-line slogan to advertise your product. Begin by writing sentences about your product. The sentences should include WHO is going to buy the product, refer to or suggest WHAT it does, and imply WHY anyone must buy it. Invent a catchy brand name.

Practice Slogans _____

_____

_____

_____

Final Slogan _____

_____

_____

_____

THE URGE TO TRAVEL

Travel literature has never been more popular than it is today. Countless magazines are devoted to articles suggesting out-of-the-way, exotic, or well-known places to vacation. Authors write entire books about their journeys. Newspapers devote weekend sections to features on vacation places. Travel writers have a way of making their readers want to visit those places they describe.

Where is the most interesting place that you have ever been? Maybe it is Tibet or maybe a pond in Sioux Falls or perhaps the top of New York City's Empire State Building. Perhaps you would choose a summer camp or your own neighborhood swimming pool. Whatever place you would choose, we all know interesting places to visit.

Your interesting place _____

The travel writer will invent a surprise opening for the article to grab the reader's attention. The article may begin with a question or a statement about a little-known bit of information. This information rouses the reader's curiosity. The article will be written with upbeat descriptions. It will only mention the most positive aspects.

Read this example of the opening of a travel article on Istanbul, Turkey.

Would you think it worth climbing to the top of three castle towers to survey what remains of Byzantium? On a clear day the wide blue sky stretches over the yet bluer Bosphorus Strait, the only body of water in the world that divides a city that straddles two continents. This glorious place is Istanbul.

Write a travel article about your interesting place. Begin with a question or surprising information. Use your most energetic way of writing. You are trying to sell your readers on this spot. Write your opening as though you were a salesperson talking.

_____

_____

_____

_____

_____

_____

_____

_____

Travel writers urge readers to travel to a particular place by designing a clear and appealing picture of it. This picture in words will include new and interesting details. These details will depict this place as a unique place.

Read this example of interesting details about Istanbul.

Simultaneously, the Bosphorus hugs the teeming shorelines of Europe and Asia on its deep and swift five-mile sweep from the Black Sea to the Marmara Sea. Then it silently pushes on to the Aegean Sea through the Dardanelles, where the ship of the mythical Odysseus was threatened by the towering rocks. The ancient city of Byzantium was later named Constantinople, and in this century, Istanbul. Still, it spreads back into the crowded hills and winding streets like a huge crown laden with jewels of every kind imaginable.

Continue your travel piece by describing the details that make your spot interesting, relaxing, or exciting. Use adjectives to make the images complete. Action words or verbs will add energy to the positive sales pitch. Try to sound as though you think your place is the best!

_____

_____

_____

_____

_____

Conclude with the impressive attractions. Be specific as to why this place is wonderful and unique. Include the sounds, colors, kinds of people, and particular smells that would entice travelers. Insert interesting information and urge your readers to go there!

_____

_____

_____

_____

Section 3

Writing Poetry

UNFOLDING POEMS

Poems are made of lines which connect ideas. Poets may not know what ideas are going to unfold until the poem develops. The action, images, and form of the poem will also unfold as the poem is written.

Poets sometimes begin writing a poem from an interesting idea or image; then they allow the ideas and images of one line to continue into the next without concern for the ending.

Study the list of words below until your imagination gives you an idea or image of *one* of the words or phrases. Use that word in the first line of your poem. The line can be a sentence or phrase. Write the line below. Do not worry if your line does not seem perfect now. You can always change it later.

- *bronze, cowbell, blaze, creek, green shadow, distances, evening*
  For example: the creek that runs by my granddaddy's farm

_____

_____

Allow your ideas and images from your first line to continue into the second line. Study the second group of words until one word continues the thought of your first line.

- *winter, pine trees, snow, breeze, meanders, wind, listener*
  For example: meanders through valleys, pours over hillsides

_____

_____

Find a word or phrase from the list below to use in your next line. In this line, the ideas and images from the first two lines will expand even more.

- *dawn, ripping, ground, horse, grazing, dip, night song, babble*
  For example: To step into the creek is to dip into a coolness.

Select a word or phrase from the next list that extends the connection.

- *summer sweat, stairs, lanterns, cold, empty hands, moon, road's edge*
  For example: when summer beats down and sweat pours like rain

---

Choose from the list to let the ideas and images continue.

- *steps, street, passing, mist, whole, nothing, fresh*
  For example: The fresh water in my mouth is grass and mint.

Select a word or phrase from the last list that will bring all the ideas and images which have developed in this poem to a closure. You can change any line as you revise later.

- *reeds, frailty, web, jostling, cattle, spoon, green eyes, woods*
  For example: jostling through other pastures to some distant girl in the flatlands

---

Read the poem below created after the example responses were written in a stanza.

> *Creek Life*
> *The creek that runs by my granddaddy's farm*
> *meanders through valleys, pours over hillsides.*
> *To step into the creek is to dip into a coolness*
> *when summer beats down and sweat pours like rain.*
> *The fresh water in my mouth is grass and mint,*
> *jostling through other pastures to some distant girl in the flatlands.*

Write your poem by arranging all your lines together just as the example poem illustrates. When you have completed your revisions, write your final draft. Remember to add a provocative title.

LINES THAT STOP IN THE MIDDLE

Poetry is divided into lines. The end of a line is called a *line break*. Although lines can consist of complete sentences, they can be incomplete phrases with the rest of the sentence on the next line. This line break technique is called *enjambment*. Read the example poem to see how enjambment works.

If Christopher Columbus broke
through the wall of waves
by following the lights
in his mind, and in the unbounded
night sky, which is fathoms deep,
can't I take this
one new plunge?

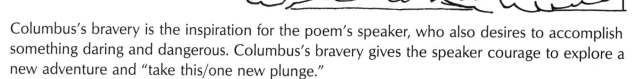

Columbus's bravery is the inspiration for the poem's speaker, who also desires to accomplish something daring and dangerous. Columbus's bravery gives the speaker courage to explore a new adventure and "take this/one new plunge."

Do you see which lines are enjambed? In fact, the example poem is one long question and each line continues onto the next for its entire meaning. The first enjambed line break gives readers several ideas or connotations. For example, it *could* mean that Columbus "broke through the wall of waves" to get to the New World. Or it *could* mean that he broke through the darkness of fear into the light of courage.

Rewrite the example Columbus poem using different line breaks. Think about how your use of different enjambment will further modify the meaning of the lines.

_____

_____

_____

_____

_____

_____

_____

_____

TALKING OBJECTS

Objects cannot speak; however, you can use a writing technique called *personification* to have objects "talk" like people. Think of an object that you use every day. Write the answers to the following questions as you analyze your object.

SIGHT: What color is your object? Does it have any special features? What is its shape? List all the parts of your object.
For example: My family's car is forest green, with coils and a tail pipe.
SOUND: Does it make a sound? What sounds are associated with it?
For example: RRRRR! and slush
TASTE: Does it need to "eat" anything to function? Any food associated with it?
For example: It eats gas.
TOUCH: What is its texture like? Do various parts feel different?
For example: slick, windshield's icy glaze
SMELL: Does your object have a special scent? Does it pick up odors from being used?
For example: mud, oil

Read the example poem written from the car's point of view. The personification emphasizes that the car is a helpful companion, but one that is often neglected. Notice how some of the words in the poem are in the examples above.

The Family Car

RRRRight!
Every morning, rain or snow,
My coils are expected
To heat up fast, get you to class on time.
Sometimes my stomach's near empty
And you forget my gassy breakfast.
My forest green body ought to shine
Like a well-groomed park,
But, this winter,
You haven't even given me a bath.
My tail pipe's coated in salt,
Wheels are caked with muddy slush,
Headlights look dazed and windshield is glazed.
Don't forget to do your homework!

Write a poem about your object and use personification. Imagine that your object can talk to you. What is its attitude? Does it appreciate or resent you? Why? Why not?

Name _____

THE MOST EXCITING HOLIDAY OF THE YEAR

Everyone looks forward to holiday times when family and friends get together for special traditions, food, and fun. Consider all of the holidays of the year. Choose the one which is your favorite and write its name below.

Favorite Holiday _____

Explain why you selected this holiday by analyzing the various events that take place during your favorite holiday. Be specific with details.

When is your favorite holiday? _____

How long is your favorite holiday? _____

What types of music or entertainment occur? _____

_____

What kind of clothing or costumes do you wear? _____

_____

What kinds of food are served during this time? _____

_____

What other activities are planned? _____

_____

_____

_____

_____

Name _____

Write a description of your favorite holiday. Use ideas from the questions you answered, as well as any thoughts you have as you write the description.

For example: July 4 is an explosive day
                one day in the summer which lets us stretch our fun
                "The Star-Spangled Banner" makes us proud
                colorful marching bands with uniforms in the streets
                in the park watermelon and hot dogs eaten
                at night fireworks swimming all day

_____

_____

_____

_____

Read the example draft poems below. Analyze how the lines used the descriptive words.

Example Draft One

  Hot and Explosive
We stretch summer fun
On the Fourth of July.
Star-spangled uniforms march
Past hot dogs and watermelon feasts.
Afternoon splashing in seas and pools.

Example Draft Two

  Hot Time
On the FOURTH day, summer fun
Stretches wide as the sun.
In every town star-spangles march.
Beaches, parks, and yards explode
With hot dogs, splashes, and watermelon feasts.
At 10:00 p.m. fireworks outglow the stars.

Example Final Draft

    Hot
On the fourth day, summer fun
Stretches wide as the sun.
In every town, star-spangles march.
Beaches, parks, and yards splash
Hot dogs, watermelon, fireworks.

Write the first draft of your poem about your selected holiday. Write a second draft. Then write your final draft, rearranging lines and deleting and adding words with each draft.

You Get Your Fingers in Everything!

Have you ever considered how much you can tell about people just by looking at their fingers? In literature, writers give clues that reveal their characters by using this type of small detail. Writers use the character's dialogue, actions, hairstyles, clothes, mannerisms, and any other detail to give clues to a character's personality.

For example, you can probably tell if someone is married by the rings worn by that person. You can see hints of age from wrinkles. From tan or roughness of a person's skin, you can guess that he or she may be a gardener or laborer. A surgeon or sculptor can have delicate, expressive hands. What about the fingernails? What do they show about a person?

1. Trace your open hand.

2. Observe your hand closely. Write all of the details that you see inside the shape you traced. Are there clues under your nails? On your nails? In the length or shape of your nails? What do these things reveal about you? What do rings, texture of your skin, color, and cuticles tell about you?

3. After you have all of this information in the outline of your hand, write a funny poem about your hand. Do not give your name away in the poem. When you are finished, share your poem with classmates. See if the clues reveal your identity.

Name _____

IMAGES OF STRANGERS

If you are observant, you can write poetry about people you really do not know. Recall a stranger you have seen at some time.

- Who was the stranger? _____
  For example: farmer, carpenter, figure skater, basketball player, bus driver

- Answer the following questions to help you remember the stranger.

1. Where did you see the stranger? _____

2. What actions describe what the stranger was doing? _____

_____

_____

3. What was interesting about the stranger's clothing? Face and hands? Speech?

_____

_____

4. What sounds were present around the stranger? Was the stranger near anything that made noise? Describe the sounds. _____

_____

_____

5. What details made the stranger unique or noticeable? _____

_____

_____

- Write a short description of the stranger. Include details, comparisons, and action words that you used in the answers to your questions.

A *metaphor* is a comparison of two things that are different. The metaphor joins one or more details to create a new idea. A common metaphor is "Your cheeks are roses." *Cheeks* and *roses* are different, but they are similar in details. Both are red in color and soft in texture.

- Write a metaphor that compares a detail of the stranger with some part of his or her description.
  For example: The farmer's hands are the grooved furrows he has plowed.

  _____

- Read the following example to see how the metaphor is used in the poem.

Sunrise
The farmer's hands are the grooved
furrows he has plowed.
Back and forth the furrows run
deeper every year.
The earth yields its richness
up to the plow and the farmer
bends to gather the ground
from the path of his plow.
It slides off his hand
through the grooves
it has helped to make.

- Write a poem that uses your metaphor about your stranger. In the example poem, the farmer's wrinkled hands remind the poet of the furrows in a plowed field. Therefore, the whole poem is about how these two different things are similar.

  _____

  _____

  _____

  _____

  _____

  _____

  _____

  _____

  _____

  _____

NAMING THE SOUNDS OF THE SCENE

Each place has its own unique sounds. It would be unusual for a garden setting to have the same sounds as a bus terminal or a circus. As you listen to sounds in a particular place, you can determine many things about that setting.

Words in a poem can describe the various sounds of a setting. When you add together all the details about the sounds in a poem, you can usually figure out the setting without it being stated directly in the poem.

Read the following example and analyze where these sounds would most likely happen.

Heat vents snore like steady steam irons
while raindrops tap on window panes,
lulling me toward napping when
a familiar voice snaps, "Louise!
Pay attention please."
Then sniffling Billy starts to tease,
tapping his ruler on his knees
just as the saving bell starts to ding.
My eyes slide through glass and rain
to watch eight buses sing again
like yellow frogs their gruff, huff
and wheeze that calls this day enough.

The accumulated sounds of "heat vents," "raindrops tap on the window panes," "Pay attention please," "tapping his ruler," "bell starts to ding," and "buses sing" all occur in the classroom setting.

To write a poem that describes sounds in a setting, select a place that you know very well. It can be as everyday as your bedroom or as special as the pier at your favorite beach.

Setting _____

With your eyes closed, imagine that you are sitting in this place. Imagine the colors, the objects, and the textures in your setting. Breathe in the scents. Listen to the sounds. There are loud or obvious sounds. However, there are soft and insignificant sounds that you may have tuned out at first.

Write about what you see and hear in your imagination about your setting. Do not be concerned about the structure of your sentences, neatness, or spelling. Those things can be corrected later. Concentrate on writing everything you imagine about your setting, using details.

_____

_____

_____

_____

_____

_____

_____

Using slash (virgule) marks (/), divide the description above into thoughts of four to eight words. _For example: The heat vents snore like steady steam irons/ while the raindrops tap on the window panes,/ lulling me toward napping when/ a familiar voice snaps, "Louise!/ Pay attention please."/_

Write the first draft of your poem by rewriting your description into lines. Use the slash marks to indicate the endings for each line.
For example: The heat vents snore like steady steam irons/
  while raindrops tap on window panes./

When you have completed your first draft, edit it. Rearrange lines, delete repetitive words, add more descriptive words, and use specific details. Make certain your poem describes the sounds in your setting so well that your readers know exactly where your poem takes place.

_____

_____

_____

_____

_____

_____

_____

_____

_____

_____

_____

PERMISSION TO EXPERIENCE THE SUBJECT

Using the five senses of sight, sound, taste, touch, and smell in description allows the reader to create a mental picture of the subject. This sensory description also allows the reader to experience the image. Through the imagination, readers experience what the writer invents for their eyes to see, ears to hear, hands to touch, tongues to taste, and noses to smell.

For example, a writer wants the reader to experience a flower. If the writer uses only the word, *flower*, the reader can understand but cannot receive an image. There are thousands of flowers of varied shapes, colors, scents, and so forth.

When a writer uses the senses to describe an iris, he or she is using description so that the reader can experience the sight and smell of the iris. Using other sensory descriptions, the reader can sometimes almost taste the freshness of the iris or feel the texture of the fragile petals.

To begin to use sensory description, choose any subject of nature that you have experienced. Limit your selection to something small, such as the iris.

Your subject _____

Add sensory description of sight.
For example: a drooping yellow iris

_____

_____

Allow your imagination to bring you up close to the subject so that you can hear, taste, and touch it.

For example: The drooping yellow iris groans with the wind under the weight of April frost.

_____

_____

_____

Fantasize that you are actually inside your subject to experience how it is.

For example: The drooping yellow iris groans with the wind under the weight of April's frost on yesterday's pleated dress, now ripped and splattered, and stiff, and ruined.

_____

_____

_____

Read the description of the iris now that all the descriptions have been put together. Notice how the slash marks divide the description into line breaks for a poem.

The drooping yellow iris groans/ with the wind/ under the weight of April's frost/ on yesterday's pleated dress,/ now ripped and splattered,/ and stiff,/ and ruined/

Place all the descriptions of your subject together as was done in the example. Then add slash marks to divide the ideas into line breaks in a poem.

_____

_____

_____

Write a poem from your description. End each line where you have placed a slash mark. Examine the following final draft, which is revised from the example descriptions of the iris.

Yesterday's Lady, Today Splattered

A drooping yellow iris groans
as spring releases her windy moans.
April's pleated dress is coated
stiff with frost, is bent and bloated.

Formula Poem

In your mind, you have many pictures or images of places you have seen. If you are an artist, you can paint a picture of these places by recalling specific details, such as colors, shapes, textures, and other particular descriptions. You can also recreate a picture of this same place by writing a poem. You *write* about the details you remember instead of painting the image.

Choose a scene you have known, one which you have visited often.
For example, a house, yard, trees, snowstorm, beach, rainy day, windy hill, or a creek

Choose your scene _____
For example: winter road

Select one object in your scene _____
For example: the mailbox on the winter road

You can write a poem which will create a picture by using specific descriptions of **what, where, actions,** and **comparisons.** The comparison you will use is called a *simile*.
For example: a mailbox is like a person with its large mouth and round tongue.

Read the *first* draft of the poem about the mailbox on the winter road. It was written as a response to the questions to its left. Notice how all the responses focus on describing the one object (the mailbox) chosen from the place (the winter road).

Mailbox on the Winter Road

1) Where is the place?	*across the road from my house*
2) What is the object?	*the mailbox*
3) What is a specific description?	*its peeping nose and eyes*
4) What colors are seen?	*black under white*
5) What is the simile (comparison)?	*like a ghost-victim*
6) What is the action?	*forcefully smothered*

You are ready to write the *first* draft of your poem. The same response questions will help you to write your first draft.

Title of your poem (name of your object and place) _____

1) Where is your place? _____

2) What is your object? _____

3) What is a specific description? _____

4) What colors do you see? _____

5) What is your simile? _____

6) What is one action in your place?_____

Here is the final draft of the example poem. Find the changes made in the example before you write your final draft.

Camouflaged

Across the road
the mailbox,
black under white,
nose and eyes peeping
like a hostage
captured by cold forces.

You noticed that words were added, deleted, or rearranged in the example poem. In your final draft, you can revise in the same ways to create a picture of your object and place.

Write your final draft below. You can change your title to something more interesting.

_____ (title)

_____

_____

_____

_____

_____

_____

_____

Acrostic Poems Are Worth a Fortune

The words in an *acrostic* poem are arranged so that the poem is read down or across. In some types of acrostic poems, the words in the title become the first word in each line, consecutively. The lines, sentences, or phrases all focus on one topic.

In the example below, the poem's title is the fortune from a Chinese cookie. You can also read the title down the left margin of the lines. The first word of each line begins a phrase that is connected to the title.

Good News Will Come from Far Away

Good-minded Grandparents will give me
News by way of the E-mail.
Will you join us in our motor home,
Come on our trip out West
From June through July?
Far from sad, I reply: Take me
Away!

Assume that you have just eaten in a Chinese restaurant, and you receive a fortune in a cookie. Select one of the following three fortunes:

- You are a bundle of energy, always on the go.
- Depart not from the path which fate has you assigned.
- Take care not to become involved in gossip.

Write your own acrostic poem from the fortune you selected.
Use the fortune you chose as your title.
Write the words in the fortune down the left-hand margin. Then finish the lines.

When you have finished, illustrate your poem.

LOOK AT THE SHAPE THINGS ARE IN

Shape poems or *concrete* poems have lines that are written so that the poem takes the form of the poem's subject matter.

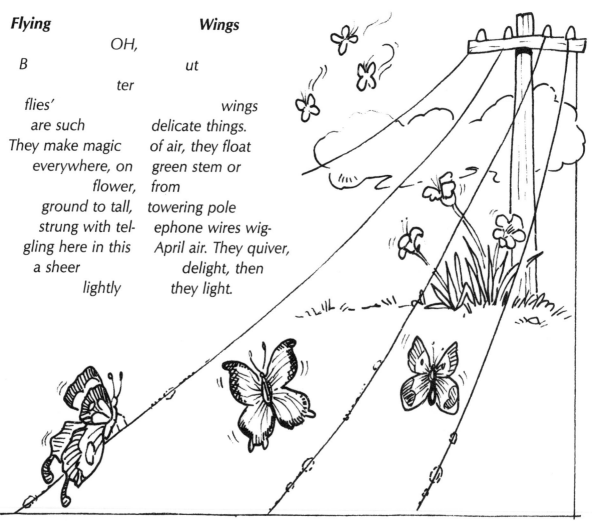

Flying

OH,

B

ter

flies'
are such
They make magic
everywhere, on
flower,
ground to tall,
strung with tel-
gling here in this
a sheer
lightly

Wings

ut

wings
delicate things.
of air, they float
green stem or
from
towering pole
ephone wires wig-
April air. They quiver,
delight, then
they light.

Picture a sailboat in your mind. What associations come to your mind when you think of a boat? Traveling to far places? Relaxing on a lake on a sunny day? Fishing? Being safe in the middle of a lot of water? Swimming? Write your ideas about boats on the back of this paper. Answer the questions in this paragraph to get you started.

Rewrite your description in the shape of the sailboat without actually drawing the shape of the sailboat. Let your words create the shape. Give your poem a title that does not give away the subject of your poem, but helps to reveal it. Study the sample poem's title as an example.

A Lovely Lyric

A *lyric* is a song-like poem that expresses a personal feeling. Read the following example.

Like the Wind

Where October winds go
shining up the fat cheeks
on waxy pumpkins
among a smoky scent of golden
soups, steamy cider spices, and toasty cinnamon,
I'll gladly go, but wait until I get my jacket.

These cheerful words show an excitement for the energy, colors, and smells of autumn. The lines move in a lyrical rhythm that is similar to the crisp October winds.

1. Choose one month of the year._____

2. List two objects that you associate with the month that you have chosen.

   _____

3. List two objects or natural elements and their smells that you associate with your month.

   _____

   _____

4. What is a general feeling you have during your month?

   _____

Write a four- to six-line lyric poem on the month you have chosen. Include the words you have already written about it. These words help you get started.

When you have finished the first draft of your poem, use the following questions to write the final draft. You can rearrange, add, and delete words or lines.
  • Do your descriptive words show the feeling you want? Do your words create pictures of sounds and smells?
  • Do the words in the lines move in a rhythm that shows the feeling?
  • Read your answer to question 4 again. Does the general feeling in your poem match your answer to that question?

COUPLETS RHYME AT THANKSGIVING TIME

Thanksgiving is the time of the year when Americans remember all of the things in life for which they are grateful. Loved ones, home, food, and clothing come to mind immediately as being some of the most obvious things to appreciate.

Name three other things for which you are thankful. For example, you could write about how appreciative you are to have learned about computer programs and the Internet.

1. _____

2. _____

3. _____

Circle one of your selections and write two sentences that explain why you are grateful to have it.

_____

_____

_____

For example: Learning computer programs lets me talk to the world. It helps me do my homework faster and shows me neat games to play.

In poetry, a rhyme is the repetition of a sound in two or more words. Rhyme that occurs at the end of a line is called *end rhyme*. A couplet is two lines together that have end rhyme.

Rewrite your sentences into a couplet. The lines must make sense, and the sounds of the final syllables must be end rhyme. They can be humorous or serious.
For example: With my computer, my homework goes fast.
It lets me talk through the air, and its games are a blast!

Write two more couplets to complete a Thanksgiving poem that is unique to you. Your finished poem will be three couplets of six lines. Add a title that pertains to Thanksgiving.

FOR YOU A HAIKU, VALENTINE

Messages on valentine cards are usually simple images and thoughts. Haiku is a type of poetry from Japan. The words in a haiku total only 17 syllables. Theses words are divided into three lines. The first and third lines contain five syllables each and the second has seven syllables. Each line can have any number of words as long as they meet the syllable requirement. In a haiku, the image is concise. There is no space for excess words.

Write the name of someone to whom you wish to send a haiku valentine._____
For example: my cousin, Jeanne

What image or place do you associate with him or her?
For example: in the green backyard by the cellar door

_____

_____

What were you thinking or feeling about him or her in this place?
For example: You were a match to fire my imagination.

_____

_____

What were the two of you doing there?
For example: weaving stories out of spiderwebs

_____

_____

Read the following first draft.

> *Jeanne, First Cousin*
> *You were a match to fire my imagination*   (12 syllables)
> *In the green backyard by the cellar door,*   (10 syllables)
> *Weaving stories out of spiderwebs.*   (9 syllables)

Begin the first draft of your own haiku.

The first line is about what you were thinking or feeling about the person you selected.

The second line is about what place or object you associate with the person.

The third line is about what the two of you were doing in that place.

Your title _____

_____

_____

_____

Count the syllables in each line of your first draft. Write the number to the right of the line as you see in the example. Eliminate or change words in your poem to make the syllables in the lines fit the formula for a haiku. Study the following revision of the example to see how syllables were eliminated so that the haiku is formed.

> *Jeanne*
> *My creative match*   (5 syllables)
> *Struck fires by the cellar door*   (7 syllables)
> *Spiderweb stories*   (5 syllables)

_____
(title)

_____

_____

_____

When you have made your final draft, send your haiku in a valentine card.

A Select Free Verse

A *free verse* poem usually does not rhyme. The lines of the poem can be of various lengths. Read the following example of a free verse poem.

Roller Skating
Slinging my legs onto the wood
and into a sound loud as
a bunch of growling beagle hounds,
I punch and pull the wind
out of my way.

Notice that the action words, *slinging, growling, punch,* and *pull* describe either the movement of a skater's arms and legs or the sound of skates on wood.

Choose a subject in the arts such as painting or dancing, or select a sport such as biking or football. Answer the questions below to help you find ideas for your subject.

- Your subject_____
  For example: roller skating

- Which parts of your body move as you perform the activity you chose?
  For example: arms or legs while skating

  _____

- How does your body move?
  For example: slinging my legs, punching and pulling my arms

  _____

- How do these actions make you feel?
  For example: tough, as if I'm saying, "Get out of my way!"

  _____

  _____

Write a five- or six-line free verse poem about your subject, using the feelings and actions you have written above. Reread the example free verse poem to get ideas. Rewrite your lines several times, finding different ways to show the actions and feelings of your subject. Then write the final draft of your poem.

ISLAND POEM

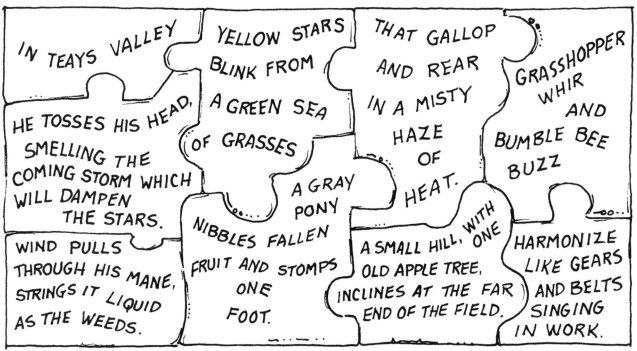

Read the poem below. As you read, visualize in your mind the pictures the words create.

The Meadow

In Teays Valley
yellow stars blink from a green sea of grasses
that gallop and rear in a misty haze of heat.
Grasshopper whir and bumble bee buzz
harmonize like gears and belts singing in work.
A small hill, with one old apple tree, inclines at the far end of the field.
A gray pony nibbles fallen fruit and stomps one foot.
Wind pulls through his mane, strings it liquid as the weeds.
He tosses his head, smelling the coming storm which will dampen the stars.

The entire poem is about one part of a larger scene. Look how each line of this poem gives some different and interesting details about this place. The lines of the poem all fit together like a puzzle to make a complete picture. This is an image poem because it creates pictures or images in the mind of the reader.

Imagine you are on an island. This island can be anywhere. It can be any kind of environment you can imagine. It can have whatever climate you wish.

Answer the following questions. Your answers may be several words or longer phrases. Do not rewrite the question. Do not write your answers in complete sentences. Write the answers to these questions as phrases in a list.

1) Where is your imagined island?
2) What is the color or texture of the surrounding water?
3) Describe the movement of the water with details of color and action.
4) Briefly describe two different sounds you can hear.
5) What does each sound like?
6) Add two details of things you can see that show the physical appearance of the island.
7) Name one object on the beach, in a field, on a mountain, or any spot on the island.
8) Show what one element of nature (snow, wind, rain, and sun) is doing.
9) Add one more detail.

After you have answered these questions, you have a rough draft of a poem about the island that you have created. Your next step is to revise these lines into the final draft of your island poem.

You can rearrange your ideas. You can add ideas as you revise. You can use new details of sight, sound, taste, smell, and touch. You are creating a poem so that your readers can imagine your island in their minds. Your poem will create a picture or an image in their minds.

_____

_____

_____

_____

_____

_____

_____

_____

_____

_____

_____

_____

_____

When you have finished your final copy, illustrate your poem.

CATEGORY POEM

Category poems focus on one area of a subject. In the contents of these poems, poets show a variety of ideas about their subjects.

For example: Subject—The Arts. Category—Music. Ideas—Fifties' rock and roll, jazz, polka, opera, hard rock, country, rhythm and blues, easy listening, Broadway musicals, hymns, classical Spanish guitar, folk, ballad, patriotic, holiday, and classic.

A poet's particular attitude toward the content is what makes the category poem unique.

In the Groove

*I'm a very unclassic dude, I am not
a Schubert see me sail away into a pink
dream whenever some Spanish guitar
plucks out in the night, and when I say Country
I do not mean a tight-laced French ballad, dig me
hot into get-down scuffling rockin' rhythm and blues.*

Follow the directions below to create your own category poem, using the category given.

The Subject: Travel. The Category: Travelers. Ideas: Imagine that you are either in an airport, a bus terminal, or a train station. It is a crowded center. There is a wide variety of people: many people coming in, moving about with their business, and leaving.

1. On notebook paper, make a list of six different types of people at the station. Skip a line between each type of person.
   For example: an older man with a child   young foreign Asian woman

2. Beside each name write words that describe how he or she looks, speaks, and behaves.
   For example: An older man with a child—suit and tie, boots, eye glasses, straight black hair, gray beard, smiled at the child, had brown and white luggage, used personal telephone, walked sluggishly, sleeping, complained about seating, read the newspaper, official clerk stamped his tickets, mumbled about plans to get a new job

You now have enough ideas about each person to write an eight- to ten-line category poem about travelers. Review your descriptions until you get an idea about the attitude you will take about travelers. Then, select from your words and write your poem.

SHORT AND SMART THINGS TO SAY IN VERSE

The *epigram*, a short poetic form, is full of wit and wisdom. The epigram is usually only two or four lines in length. It is written in couplets (two rhyming lines) or a quatrain (four alternating rhyming lines).

Epigrams have been around since ancient times and are still widely written today. These poems often depend on *satire*, which is a sharp or humorous attack on current issues such as politics or social standards. The following are several examples.

He had a burning belief in the right to smoke
Until he ran out of fire after his stroke.

The rich deduct taxes for donations and business events
While the working man and woman are left with no cents.

Invention and progress are bound to be steady
As long as man and womankind continue their course;
But the course won't be long unless they're ready
To respect the environment, the most important force.

For your epigram, choose a current topic of debate that you have recently read about or heard discussed by the media. The topic you choose may be any subject, such as political matters, social fads, moral or religious standards, or different opinions within your school or family.

Example: Should people of all ages have the right to smoke when and where they wish?

Your topic: _____

List the pros and cons of the issues regarding the topic for your epigram.
Example: Everyone should be free to choose to smoke; tobacco causes cancer, heart attack, stroke; it is addictive; young people particularly should be prohibited from starting.

Your pro and con issues _____

_____

_____

_____

List on the lines below, the types of people who are involved in the issues of your topic.
Example: politicians, youth, adults, manufacturers, farmers, tobacco merchants

_____

_____

You are now ready to write your epigram. Complete the following step-by-step process.

1) Select one of the people you listed above.

2) Next, select one of the issues pertaining to the topic. Make certain the issue is directly connected to the person you selected. If necessary, change either the person or the issue.

3) Write a couplet (a two-line epigram) or a quatrain (a four-line epigram).

4) Add satire to your lines. Reread the description and examples of satire.

Write your first drafts and your final draft. Read your final epigram aloud.

_____

_____

_____

_____

_____

_____

_____

_____

_____

_____

_____

A Long-Lasting Verse

Have you ever gone into an old cemetery and read the verses written on the tombstones? It is interesting to reflect on words that make a comment about the death of someone. The verse found on tombstones is called an *epitaph*.

Even though an epitaph is a poem about someone who has died, it is not always placed on a gravestone. It can be placed anywhere. Some can be found in books or on walls. It may be serious or sad, but more often, it is comic. Some epitaphs have puns. When a pun is used, the author is "playing on a word" so that the word takes on two different meanings at the same time.

Below are epitaphs found on old tombstones. The authors are unknown. Notice how the anonymous writers use puns and humor.

Here lies what's left
Of Leslie Moore.
No Les,
No more.

Here lies one blown out of breath,
Who lived a merry life, and died a Merideth.

Follow the steps 1-4 to prepare to write an epitaph.

1. Make up a name. *Example: Leslie Moore.*

   Name: _____

2. Break the name into syllables to see if there are several smaller words within the name. *Example: Les, lie*

   _____

3. Look for puns in the sounds of the name. *Example: Moore/more; Les/less*

   _____

4. If you do not have basic material for an epitaph after doing 1-3, go back and make up another name. You may have to do this several more times until you are ready to write your verse. Then write your epitaph.

Once you have written your epitaph, draw a tombstone. Then transpose your epitaph onto it.

POEMS OF COMMON SENSE AND NONSENSE

Limerick poetry is always humorous. The rhyme patterns and rhythm in limericks are always the same:

> The first two lines rhyme and have seven or eight syllables.
> The next two lines rhyme and have five or six syllables.
> The last line rhymes with the first two lines and has nine or ten syllables.

Commonly, limericks depend on double meanings, pronunciation, or peculiarities in spelling for the trick that makes them humorous and fun. These poems tackle any subject, such as the following examples by unknown authors.

An epicure dining at Crewe
Found a large mouse in his stew.
Said the waiter, "Don't shout
And wave it about,
Or the rest will be wanting one too!"

A housewife called with a frown
When surprised by callers from town,
"In a minute or less
I'll slip on a dress"—
But she slipped on the stairs and came down.

Write your own limerick. Choose one of the following ideas. Of course, you may use your own idea.

> A dog looking for its master
> A rooster who would not crow
> The soldier who hid behind a tree
> One who will not get up from bed in the mornings
> A man who sings in the shower
> A child who got on the wrong bus

_____

_____

_____

_____

_____

_____

Once you have mastered the form, try writing limericks about characters found in literature, social studies, sports, the arts, and even science—or the world of entertainment.

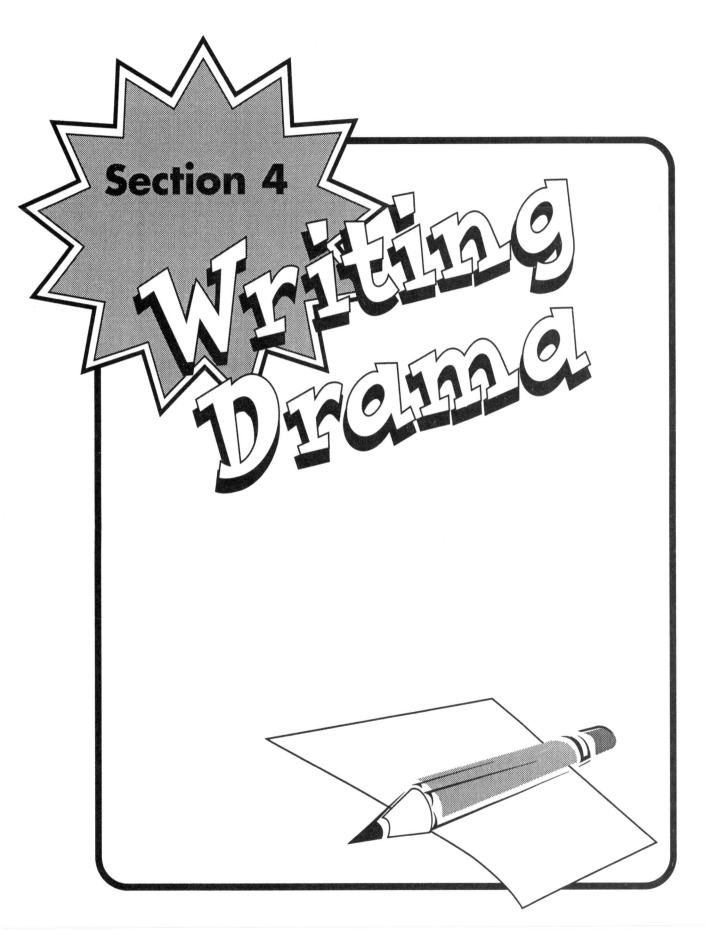

Section 4

Writing Drama

Get Ready, Get Set, Go On with the Show

The set depicts the setting of the play. The action can take place anywhere—outdoors, in a room, on a battlefield, or in a ballroom. The set includes all objects on stage and the scenery that is built or painted to represent the environment.

Choose from one of the settings listed below or invent one of your own.

> an old graveyard overgrown with weeds from years of neglect
> a modern and expensively furnished kitchen
> a field in a valley where a battle will take place
> a street in a large city
> a large and open porch on a country house with a wide yard
> a ballpark
> the main room of a library

Your selection: _____

The set helps the audience imagine the environment surrounding the action of the play.

Draw the setting that you selected. Construct the details—the walls, the trees, the outside cityscape. Add the properties—those are items on the set that can be moved around, such as chairs, tables, and lamps. Everything on your set is important to help the audience understand the play.

When you have completed your drawing, write a paragraph describing your set. Include in your paragraph all of the important details of scenery and properties in your drawing.

Name _____

IMPORTANT PROPERTIES

Properties, or *props* as they are called in the theater, are always important to the play. They can even be symbolic and represent a main idea of the play. For example, a beautifully decorated Christmas tree can symbolize a happy family. That same tree can symbolize an unhappy family if it becomes shaggy and tattered as the play progresses. The Christmas tree is a prop, but it is also a symbol in the play for the seemingly happy family falling apart.

Read the following summary of a scene from a play.

In winter, the wind howls around a run-down farmhouse. The clock strikes midnight in this scene's darkened living room, full of shabby furnishings. An old man, leaning on a cane, shuffles in from the back. He pauses, looks long at a picture sitting on an end table. Then, he thumps, one step at a time, toward the fireplace. With great effort, he stirs up the fire that is almost going out. He turns again toward the picture and picks it up. It is of a young bride. He studies it. Finally, he leans back, drags a tattered quilt across his chest, and closes his eyes, hugging the picture under the quilt. The wind howls again.

1. Underline all of the props in this scene.

2. Are the props related? _____ What do they symbolize?

   _____

   _____

3. There is the atmosphere of midnight, winter, and a fire almost gone out. How are the props and atmosphere related? _____

   _____

   _____

4. Who do you think is the bride in the picture? _____

5. What feeling or idea do the properties and atmosphere represent? _____

   _____

   _____

   _____

Read another stage description.

In a backyard, a girl named Betsy takes turns blowing soap bubbles through small plastic wands with two friends, Lindsay and Dorrie. They joyfully chase the bubbles, which shine like rainbows in the sunlight. Betsy pauses to watch, then turns and looks toward the porch of the house. She resumes playing and follows some bubbles to the fence. The other two run out of the gate and off stage. Betsy looks down at a large daffodil and picks it. She turns with it and runs toward the house. There is a shadow waving to her at the window.

1. What do the bubbles, rainbows, and flowers symbolize?

   _____

Choose a place you have known, such as a porch, yard, attic, river, or cellar. When you have selected a scene, think about the answers to the following questions.
   1. What season is it? What is the atmosphere of this scene? Its weather and sounds?
   2 What are the colors? The shapes?
   3. Who is there? What activities are the characters doing? Who is the main character? What emotion is the main character feeling?
   4. Imagine two props in this scene. These two props should symbolize what is happening in the scene and represent the emotions of the main character.

Write a detailed summary of this scene. Describe this setting, its atmosphere, the characters, and the action. Include in your description the two symbolic props and their uses.

Write a final draft and have other students act it out.

_____   _____

_____

_____

_____

_____

_____

_____

_____

_____

_____

_____

_____

_____

Name _____

Wearing the Right Costume

You would not expect an actor playing the part of a salesperson to be dressed in a clown's outfit. Nor would you think it normal to see an actor in the role of a teenager with gray hair and a cane. However, such costumes for these roles could be called for if the reasons for them were written into the script.

Usually, predictable costumes fit the characters' roles. Furthermore, just as you can tell a lot about various people in your town by the way they dress, costumes in theater reveal much about characters. Sometimes bright colors, like red, will be worn to represent an outgoing personality. Dark colors, like black, may symbolize the evil or very serious.

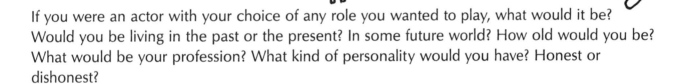

If you were an actor with your choice of any role you wanted to play, what would it be? Would you be living in the past or the present? In some future world? How old would you be? What would be your profession? What kind of personality would you have? Honest or dishonest?

What role would you like to play? _____

Imagine yourself playing the role you chose. Your costume would most likely reveal many aspects of who you are, such as a profession, outlook on life, sense of style, introverted or extroverted personality, and even some sloppy or neat habits. The colors, fads, accessories, and hairstyles you would wear show the character you would play.

Write a description of the costume your character would wear. Be detailed and specific. If your character is wearing something that is out of character, explain why in your description.

_____

_____

_____

_____

_____

WRITE THE RIGHT NAME AND YOU WON'T GO WRONG

An author who writes plays is called a *dramatist* or *playwright*. A drama basically intends to portray and reveal characters who have struggles, discoveries, successes, and failures with life. The playwright names the characters with special care so that the name "fits" the role.

For example, one of America's finest dramatists, Eugene O'Neill, named three of the sailors on a tramp steamer in his 1922 play, *Bound East for Cardiff*, Driscoll, Cocky, and Scotty. Cocky is described as a "wizened runt of a man" who often speaks "indignantly." Driscoll is described as "a brawny Irishman with the battered features of a prizefighter." Scotty is "a dark young fellow" who is rather sarcastic.

Invent five names and write them on the left-hand lines below.

_____   _____

_____   _____

_____   _____

_____   _____

_____   _____

On the line to the right of each of your names, write a phrase that describes the image that comes to your mind when you focus on the name.
For example: Cocky   a wizened runt of a man

In the opening scene of ONeill's 1922 play, his three sailors are all in a compartment on a British tramp steamer. It is sailing through the foggy night on its way from New York to Cardiff. O'Neill describes their bunk beds, the portholes, benches, lamps, chests, objects, and the floor so that a reader can know how the scene is arranged. He also states where the men are in the scene and what they are doing as the scene opens.

Imagine that you are a playwright and that your three characters are together in the play's opening scene. Consider their names and descriptions. Where would these five different characters be together?

Setting: _____

Describe an opening scene with your characters and setting. What does your scene look like as the curtain first opens? As the lights come up, describe any props that might be used by the characters. What smells and sounds would be perceived as the scene progresses? Where are your characters located on the stage? What are they doing? The opening scene takes only 10-20 seconds, but the playwright must write it clearly so that the scene can be reproduced on stage.

_____
_____
_____
_____
_____
_____
_____
_____
_____
_____

Name _____

THE IMAGINARY TIME MACHINE

What if the time machine were not imaginary? What if one morning you woke up and a time machine sat in your room? It was running, just waiting for you to jump in for a ride to the past. Where would you want to go? To what time period would you want to go?

Imagine that you have powers to go back in the past and change something that happened in history. You can change a large event such as a war or a small event such as the Super Bowl championship. What would you want to change? How would you make the change? What obstacles would you encounter? Who would help you cause this change?

Write a scene in which you and a person from the past discuss how you are going to cause this change. Dialogue in a play sounds the same as everyday conversations.

SPEAKER ONE

SPEAKER TWO

SPEAKER ONE

SPEAKER TWO

SPEAKER ONE

You will need to continue your dialogue on a separate page to complete your dialogue.

FINDING A SOLUTION

A *solution* is an acceptable outcome to a problem. In our daily lives we are constantly finding ways to work out difficulties. In a play, characters have complicated problems.

Read the example synopsis. A *synopsis* is a brief summary paragraph that explains the main ideas, characters, and problems in the play. This synopsis stops at the middle of the problem rather than revealing the solution.

Synopsis
SUMMER UPSET (title)
Characters:
   Laura: average 17-year-old teen
   Mom: Laura's mother
   Quinn: Laura's four-year-old brother
   Dad: Laura's father
   Sally: Laura's friend who is 18-19 years old

(synopsis) Laura hopes someday to be a teacher. She is active in school choir, band, clubs, and other activities. The teen finally talks her parents into allowing her to apply for her first job as an intern/assistant to the music director of a six-week summer camp in a neighboring county. Laura is hired, goes to the camp, and becomes happily successful at the camp. During her first week, she has made a new friend with Sally, an assistant counselor from another state. At the end of that week, by telephone, Laura's dad informs Laura that her mother needs to have an operation soon. Mother doesn't want to have the operation because it will mean that Laura must come home to take care of her four-year-old brother, Quinn, while her mother gets well. That night, Laura and Sally have the following exchange of words. (Conversation in a play is called *dialogue*.)

SALLY: It's not right for them to make you give up your summer.

LAURA: (*sadly*) But it's my family, my mom!

SALLY: (*forcefully*) Tell them you need this training for your future, and that they should hire a nurse.

LAURA: (*tearfully*) If I leave, I'll miss this great opportunity, but if I don't, I'll feel guilty about letting my family down.

Can you find a solution for Laura and her family? The problem must be solved in some satisfactory way, even if the solution does not make every one of the characters happy. When you have found a solution, write your synopsis.

_____

_____

_____

_____

Now that you have written a summary of the solution, write a dialogue between Laura and Dad as they talk on the phone. It should involve your solution.

LAURA: _____

_____

_____

DAD: _____

_____

_____

LAURA: _____

_____

_____

DAD: _____

_____

_____

LAURA: _____

_____

_____

Finish this dialogue on another sheet of paper. Read your finished dialogue aloud. What were the solutions?

TALKING IT OVER WITH YOURSELF

Plays are stories acted out on a stage, and the characters generally use dialogue to communicate. However, some plays include *monologue*, which means that a character talks to himself or herself. During a monologue, the audience is listening to a character think aloud. A monologue may be funny or serious. The character may or may not be alone on stage. Sometimes other characters overhear the monologue; sometimes they do not.

Example:
Rodney: Did you hear what she just said? She actually said she would dance with me! Mom was right. It is really cool to come to a dance. I was just sure this dance was going to be so boring. Well, I was wrong. This is all too good to be true, but I don't want to wake up just yet. Here comes Amber back from the punch bowl, and it looks like they are playing our song. She really meant she would dance with me!

Think about something that happened to you in the past two weeks. Imagine this event as a play in which you are one of the main characters.

Select an event from your past two weeks.

_____

Write a sentence about what happened.

_____

_____

Divide the events of this story into six sections.

1. How did it begin? _____

_____

_____

2. Who was there? _____

_____

_____

3. What happened? _____

_____

_____

_____

4. What was a surprise, shock, disappointment, change, or problem that occurred?

_____

_____

_____

5. What action then resulted? _____

_____

_____

6. How did the event end? _____

_____

_____

Write a monologue about your event. In the monologue, analyze what it was like to be in this situation. Make certain it sounds as though you are thinking aloud about what happened to you.

_____

_____

_____

_____

_____

_____

_____

_____

_____

_____

_____

_____

_____

IN THE SPOTLIGHT

A *soliloquy* is a speech that reveals the innermost thoughts or feelings of a character in a play. Have you ever felt your school year is similar to a play in which you are the central character? How do you like the role you play?

Imagine you are on a stage playing you at school. In one of the scenes, step away from the other characters and go down to the edge of the stage. The lights darken. Only one spotlight stays on, and it falls on you. You begin to speak directly to the audience about this one scene. You are giving a soliloquy.

For example: Soliloquy Subject: Loosing Out on Winning the Spelling Bee

<u>I should have at least made the finals.</u> Memorizing is easy for me, and I don't mind being in the spotlight. For weeks, when they talked about it and told us to study, I did. I studied enough for the rest of my life and imagined myself when it was my turn to spell something like hijacked or imprisonment. I would break into a knowing smile when the others failed to spell correctly. <u>Little did I suspect</u> I would never be the one to step proudly up to the podium as the dignitary called a name. <u>It wouldn't be mine</u>. The way I was studying every night made me <u>all too sure</u> the winning certificate was already in my hands. <u>But I hadn't counted</u> on coming down with the virus that would keep me at home with a fever.

Your soliloquy may be about your relationship with someone, about an event, a school subject, a problem, an accomplishment, or any other event at school.

Name the subject of your soliloquy. _____

Analyze your attitude about your subject. How do you feel about it? Why? What specific event happened in regard to your subject? Describe this scene concerning your subject. How did it affect your thoughts and feelings at the time? How does it affect you now?

Your analysis_____

_____

_____

_____

_____

_____

_____

Write your soliloquy as though you were giving a heart-to-heart confession to a sympathetic friend. Your thoughts and feelings have a particular tone. *Tone* is your manner of expressing your attitude toward your subject. Your choice of words will determine the tone of the speech. The tone can be light, harsh, humorous, serious, complaining, or any other tone. Reread the example soliloquy before you begin. Why are certain phrases underlined?

_____

_____

_____

Notice that the underlined words help the soliloquy establish a tone of disappointment. See how the speaker is revealing his or her innermost feelings about the spelling bee.

Reread your analysis about your subject, then write your soliloquy.

_____

_____

_____

_____

_____

_____

_____

_____

_____

_____

_____

_____

_____

_____

_____

_____

Name _____

A Spring Holiday Creation of Mime

Pantomime or *mime* is a form of drama that uses body movements and facial expressions instead of words. The mime artists, Charlie Chaplin and Marcel Marceau, were known throughout the modern world for the many short and silent stories they portrayed.

If you were looking out a large picture window in the springtime, you would see many signs of nature coming to life. Though you may not hear the sounds of the activities, you could watch the new season unfold before your eyes. With your imagination, you could see more of the hidden and developing springtime life.

Choose an activity from the list below or choose your own springtime activity.

1. An earthworm digging up through the wet earth breaks through topsoil to the air.
2. A tree in blossom caressed, tickled, and sways in the playful wind.
3. A bud on a long stem unfolds itself in slow-motion becoming a flower.
4. The robin busily builds a nest and finally sits in it to lay eggs.
5. A lone snake crawls out of its hole and explores its environment.

Read the example to get ideas for a description of your activity.

New Chick

Fuzzy, yellow feathers curled into a ball; small beak buried in its stomach is sleeping in warm dark liquid. Tiny claws on two thin legs clinch. Minute jerks, eyes closed, it turns its head and tries to stretch. Claws hit a barrier. Chick fidgets, moves its head through the liquid, and hits the wall. It shakes its head and flexes a spindly claw. As it pulls its head back, the beak hits the barrier with a clack. The chick gets an idea and hits with the beak again and again. It is startled when it hears a loud splitting crack that brings a bit of light to smack its closed eyes. It pecks harder and harder until it has a hole. It chips relentlessly at the hole, pushing through. The shell cracks open and falls away. Standing wobbly, opening eyes, the proud chick ruffles its wings in the sunshine.

From this description a mime would use body movements, facial expressions, and gestures of the chick to show the audience what is happening.

Write a description of the activity you chose. Use enough details that a mime could perform the short silent story after reading it. Check back to the example to see how movement was described.

Section 5

Speech Writing

OPPOSITES ATTRACT

One of the most thought-provoking writing techniques is the *oxymoron*. Using two words together that have opposite meanings causes readers to go back for a second look. For example, the oxymoron, "passive resistance" was utilized by Mahatma Gandhi to change the social structure in India. The word *passive* alone denotes inaction, but when combined with *resistance*, an active response, a new idea emerges. Though Gandhi was nonviolent, he was extremely active and forceful. The "passive resistance" movement was a successful civil rights movement in the 1960s in the United States.

Select a well-known person from the past or present.

Well-known person _____
For example: Marilyn Monroe

Write one word which describes an obvious characteristic of this person.
For example: flamboyant

Obvious characteristic: _____

Choose a second obvious characteristic of this person that is the direct opposite of the first characteristic above.
For example: insecure

Second characteristic: _____

Change the ending of your two words if necessary to make them fit together to create an oxymoron.
For example: insecurely flamboyant

Oxymoron _____

Describe your person. Focus on analyzing his or her two differing characteristics.
For example:

Flamboyant—loved to perform before the public. Was a beauty known for bleached blonde hair and bright red lips. Looked comfortable doing unexpected actions to get publicity. Was a loved and popular actress all over the world.

Insecure—she always needed to be in a romantic relationship to feel loved. Felt she was never good enough. Thought the public did not take her acting seriously.

Describe the first characteristic of your person. _____

_____

_____

Describe the second characteristic of your person. _____

_____

_____

Write a speech about your person. Begin your speech by presenting your oxymoron in the first two sentences. Explain the two opposite characteristics in the body of your speech. Include specific details. Conclude your speech with a brief statement that refers back to your oxymoron.

Present your speech without stating your person's name. Let the class guess the identity by secret ballot.

IRONICALLY SPEAKING

Irony is a literary term. It presents a situation in which events turn out to be the exact opposite of what is expected. Irony can be humorous or quite serious.

Read the following example of irony.

My sister, Eve, was known as the style queen of the school, but on the night of the big dance, a sudden rain ruined her hair and gown. She had to put her hair in a ponytail and wear last year's gown. Ironically, since she didn't have to be concerned with being the best dresser, she ended up being so relaxed that she danced the night away having the most outstanding time of her life.

What Eve thinks will be the worst night of her life turns out to be great. The evening is just the opposite of what she expects. Eve's story shows irony.

Write a speech about a family story that is ironic. Embellish your speech with lots of descriptive details to make it more interesting.

For example, if the story about Eve were written into a narrative speech, examples of the activities Eve did to be stylish would enhance the irony of what happened. Details of her elaborate preparations for the dance and a descriptive picture of how she looked before AND after the rain would make the disaster vivid. Action and dialogue during the rain storm would also enliven the story, drawing listeners into it. All of these details help to make the final irony seem true to life.

Give your finished speech in class and compare family stories. What did you find to be true about other families and the situations that occur in all families?

EXPLAINING THE PROCESS

Through the years you have learned to do hundreds of activities from brushing your teeth or making a sandwich to playing a musical instrument or competing in a difficult sport.

Every successful activity depends on a process or system.

Choose an activity you are able to perform step-by-step. Your choices are common daily chores or activities, or outstanding or unusual accomplishments.

Your choice: _____

Explain the step-by-step process of your activity.

Write a speech about the process of completing this activity. Include and check off the following suggestions as you incorporate them into your speech.

_____ Explain your activity. What is it? Why is it important, interesting, fun, or difficult?

_____ Explain the order of your steps. Name, define, and describe how each step must be done.

_____ Close your speech by expounding on the rewards this particular activity gives to you.

Example: One task I do every day is feed my horse. It is important for me to complete this chore daily. My horse depends on me for his food, and my family relies on me to be responsible.

When I get to the barn, I usually greet my horse, Rocky, with a carrot. While he is eating his carrot, I place grain in his bucket and lay two flakes of hay in his manger. My last step is to check his water. I fill the water trough to the top.

The relationship I have with my horse is very special. He provides me with hours of fun on the trail, and I give him the food he loves to eat. We help each other have a happy life.

When you have completed your speech, read it aloud to a partner. Next, give it a title. Then, without giving hints, ask your partner to tell you why your activity sounds important, fun, interesting, or difficult. Ask your partner to repeat the steps of your activity. Incorporate changes in the revision of your speech, depending on the responses of your partner.

PERSUADING OTHERS TO MIND THEIR MANNERS

A person with good manners exhibits behavior that is socially acceptable. Positive actions and language help us to be comfortable in our associations among others. Do you wish you could say something to persuade everyone to behave more thoughtfully?

List five ways of being polite to others.

1. _____

2. _____

3. _____

4. _____

5. _____

On the other hand, bad manners are opposite behaviors to those you listed. To be in the company of bad manners makes most people feel uncomfortable. List five behaviors you consider to be rude.

1. _____

2. _____

3. _____

4. _____

5. _____

Giving a speech on the subject of manners is an effective way to share your feelings. Specific explanations of why you have formulated your opinions can help to persuade your listeners.

Choose one example of either good or bad manners from your lists.

On the lines below, write the first draft of your speech. Check off each idea as you use it in your speech.

_____ an explanation of the behavior

_____ an example of the behavior

_____ several examples of possible results of the behavior

_____ an example of the opposite behavior

_____ an example of the result of the opposite behavior

_____ a final statement of how this behavior affects the actions and feelings of others

_____

_____

_____

_____

_____

_____

_____

_____

_____

_____

_____

_____

_____

_____

_____

_____

_____

When you finish, read it aloud. Discover ways to make it more forceful, organized, clear, and specific. Do not forget concrete details!

An Address with a Symbol

Abstract nouns naming feelings, such as *love*, *unity*, *loyalty*, and *hate* communicate only a general idea of their meaning. Symbols can represent specific meanings of vague words.

A person who gives a speech often uses symbols. When speakers address large audiences, they must use language that is clearly understood. Symbols are effective tools to present ideas. Powerful emotions are attached to most symbols.

Think of three organizations that you know. Write them in column A. In column B, write a word that stands for a feeling generally associated with the organization. In column C, write the name of an object (a symbol) that represents the organization.

A. Organization	B. Feeling Associated with It	C. Symbol That Represents It
Example: Boy Scouts	*friendship*	*a knot in a rope*
_____	_____	_____
_____	_____	_____
_____	_____	_____

Imagine that you are going to address an audience. You are to inform them of the importance of one of the organizations you listed above.

Choose one of the organizations you listed. What are some of the facts you know about your organization?

_____
_____
_____
_____
_____
_____
_____
_____
_____
_____
_____

Why do the feelings about the organization exist?

_____

_____

Describe the organization's symbol. Tell any facts you know or associate with it.

For example: A knot could represent the Boy Scouts. The Boy Scouts is a place to form tight friendships. A knot is thought of as something tight.

_____

_____

_____

Write the first draft of your speech. Begin with the words from your notes that are the most interesting. Use all of your notes, but do not hesitate to add new ideas. Show why the symbol represents the organization's importance.

_____

_____

_____

_____

_____

_____

_____

_____

_____

_____

_____

_____

_____

_____

_____

Present your speech to the class.

NEVER SPEECHLESS

Nobel Peace Prize winner, Martin Luther King, Jr., was the founder of the Nonviolent Human and Civil Rights Movement. In the early 1960s, he led a freedom movement all across the United States. The goal he desired was to ensure that citizens of all races, creeds, and colors should have equal opportunities under the law. Dr. King was famous for his ability to rally crowds with his many inspiring speeches.

In a speech, one person is communicating to many people. It is written about one main idea or theme, and it is informative and exciting. The speaker usually has several points to make about the one main idea or theme.

On August 28, 1963, on the steps of the Lincoln Memorial Monument, Martin Luther King, Jr., gave one of his most famous speeches. Thousands of participants listened, in the first large integrated protest march in Washington, D.C. With his speech, "I Have a Dream," Dr. King spoke of a vision of freedom for all mankind, his main idea. The vision was that one day all Americans would

1. have the freedoms granted to them by the Constitution,
2. enjoy racial togetherness,
3. "Let freedom ring," so that
4. all Americans would be "free at last!"

There were many who believed in Dr. King's "Dream." They struggled and sacrificed to make this vision come true. In the end, Dr. King gave his life for his dream.

What ideals do you believe? Are they important? Would you struggle for them? Sacrifice?
Name three important ideas for which you would work or fight.

_____   _____   _____

Choose one of your ideas. List at least three reasons why your chosen idea is significant.

_____   _____

_____   _____

Write a speech about the idea you have chosen. Imagine that you must prepare to speak to a
large group of people whom you wish to inspire. Your goal is to convince this audience to
believe in the idea you have selected.

In your speech, you must describe at least three points. Include specific examples and details,
just as Dr. King did in his speech.

Write an interesting title for your speech. Why do you think Dr. King entitled his speech "I
Have a Dream" rather than something such as "My Vision"?

_____

_____

_____

_____

_____

_____

_____

_____

_____

_____

_____

_____

_____

_____

_____

_____

_____

_____

Section 6

Expository Writing

You Should Read This Book

Have you read any good books lately? Or have you read one in the past year that was unusual, interesting, or exciting? When we discover something good, we usually like to share our opinions about it.

Your friends are not necessarily going to read a book simply because you say it is good. *Good* is a vague opinion word. However, you could use friendly persuasion. When you make a report that includes facts and relates specific information, you are more likely to persuade others to read your book.

Write the name of a book that you have read and enjoyed. Write the author's name too.

Book _____ Author _____

Answer the following questions to organize your ideas. If you are specific, your answers will help you write a persuasive book report.

What is the main idea, focus, or theme of your book?
For example: Wit and determination overcame the difficulties of a family during the American Westward Movement of the 1800s.

_____

_____

_____

Who is the central character of the book? How would you describe the physical, mental, and emotional characteristics of this person?
For example: The main character is a 15-year-old boy named Josh. He is the oldest of five children traveling with his parents in a covered wagon. Josh is tall and strong, with keen blue eyes and stringy blond hair that reaches to his neck. He has taught himself to read and write, and he is fast at figuring out problems. Josh believes in taking actions to protect his younger brothers and sisters. Josh has courage.

_____

_____

_____

_____

_____

Are there other important characters in the story? Who are they and what do they do?
For example: There is Maria, Josh's little sister. She is smart and really admires her big brother. The wagon master is also Josh's friend. He gives Josh some responsibility and special privileges, such as letting him ride at the head of the wagon train.

_____

_____

_____

What makes your book so interesting or exciting?
For example: It has many action scenes. I can't wait to see what happens. I feel as if I am there on the plains. It gives lots of information about that period of history.

_____

_____

Give one example of a scene that was outstanding. Write some of the details.
For example: One night the wagons were circled around the campfire, and the cook was telling a story. The sky was filled with stars and everything seemed fine. Then Josh heard his five-year-old sister, Maria, screaming. She had gone to the wagon to get a shawl. Josh took a burning stick from the fire and ran back to the wagon. A large wolf had cornered Maria. Josh drove the wolf out of the camp, chasing it back into the nearby hills while waving the burning stick at it.

Example: _____

_____

Details: _____

_____

Who tells the story in the book or who is the narrator?
For example: The wagon train guide is the narrator.

_____

What is the narrator's point of view; in other words, what can the narrator see and hear?
For example: The guide sees everybody's struggle, but he is Josh's friend.

_____

_____

Write a report about the book you selected, using the information from your answers. The concrete details and specific examples in your answers enable you to write a persuasive report about your book.

Two Thumbs Up!

Almost everyone has been to see a movie at one time or another. Whether you have been to the movie theater or rented a video for your television, all of us today are movie critics.

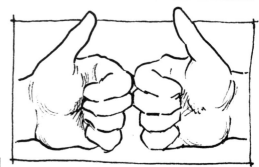

Reflect on a movie you have recently seen. How would you rate it? Was it a great movie? Or was it just "okay"? Or maybe you really thought it was bad. Gene Siskell and Roger Ebert make a living with their weekly "thumbs up, thumbs down" critiques of just-released movies. This time it is your turn. In the Siskell and Ebert tradition, which way do the thumbs point for the movie you saw?

Example: *A new film,* Winds of the South, *has just hit the movie theaters. This movie is a blockbuster! Not only does it tell a gripping story of a family's love, but it also portrays the devastation of the Deep South during the Civil War. The director fills the screen with beautiful parties on the manicured lawns of southern plantations and with the bombed out, burning Atlanta after General Sherman's march. The leading actors, Ryan Gifford and Sally Simons, make the characters, Sam Blackburn and Tippy Manly, come alive throughout their struggle for survival. In one dynamic scene, Sam courageously saves his wife, Tippy, from the burning house. This is one movie not to miss. The ending will bring tears to your eyes, making up for the length of the film. Although the movie should have been shortened by about 40 minutes, I give this one two thumbs up.*

Write your review. Use the back of this sheet if necessary.

_____

_____

_____

_____

_____

_____

_____

_____

_____

_____

PASSING NOTES

In the classroom, you may whisper a comment to a neighbor across the aisle. Your neighbor may whisper a reply. You may sometimes pass a note that asks a favor or gives information. Even though the whispered comment or the passed note had to be brief, you were communicating.

Communicating with notes means that the sender must first give information in a way that the receiver can understand.

1. Write a note to someone in class asking a question. Try to think of a question that your receiver will have to consider carefully before answering. During the note-passing, you cannot talk out loud. You can only "talk" in the note.
2. Pass the note to the receiver.
3. The receiver writes a response to your question.
4. Pass the note back to the sender.
5. Read the note. If the explanation is not clear, write another question. Pass the note back to the same receiver.
6. Continue this process until all questions are answered completely.

Read the notes aloud and discuss whether or not the explanations are complete.

TO SAY SOMETHING NICE

Receiving greeting cards always makes anyone feel appreciated. Although greeting cards are popular during holidays and other special occasions, the surprise of getting a card for no special occasion at all is exceptionally nice.

Choose someone for your special greeting.

What is your person's name? _____

What things has this person done that make you appreciate him or her? _____

_____

_____

_____

What has your special person said that impressed you?_____

_____

_____

_____

Write a two- to four-line note to the person you chose. Include the nice things you listed above. When you finish, find a blank greeting card or note paper. Copy your lines and then send it to the person you chose.

_____

_____

_____

_____

_____

_____

_____

_____

_____

_____

Thinking of You

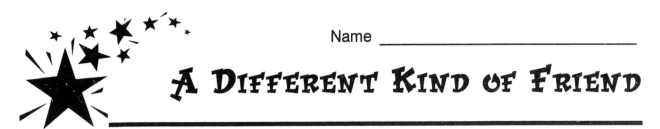

A Different Kind of Friend

During your lifetime, you have had many friendships with people. Friends are for fun, fellowship, trusting, sharing, and learning. We all need them, but a really good friend is one who will stick by you when things are not going well for you.

Have you ever had a hairy, scaly, feathered, or furry friend that you could cuddle or nuzzle? A pet with whom you could share secrets and quiet time?

Chances are that you have known an animal, bird, or reptile that you treasured. Perhaps you have one now. Pets can give us pleasure for reasons other than their compassion. Can you think of some reasons why people like to have pets?

Think of a pet. What is it about its appearance that delights you? What have you learned from it? Does it do any work? What kind of care does it need? Does it show its feelings? Does it care about its owners in a special way? What else?

Describe the pet. Be certain to explain specifically what knowing this pet means. Include a true or an imaginary story about your pet to illustrate your point.

_____

_____

_____

_____

_____

_____

_____

_____

_____

_____

_____

_____

THE REPORTER'S "FIVE AND ONE"

All newspaper articles contain the "Five Ws." They are *who, what, when, where,* and *why.* The "one" refers to *how.* Answers to the "five and one" provide clear information that readers can quickly understand.

Study this first sentence from a paragraph of an imagined newspaper sports article. *When she was young, the champion, Sherri Skymart, perfected the skills of hockey as one of the only females on ice.*

Who is the subject of the article? What is she doing? When did she begin? Where does she play? Why did she need to learn the rules early?

All of the answers to these questions can be understood from one sentence! How she plays hockey is included in the remainder of the article.

Sherri grew up in Grooms Corner, New York, a small town near Schenectady. She was the youngest of five children. The other four were boys. Her mother, Mattie Skymart, happened to be the park and recreation director for the town. During the summer, Mattie was the area's outstanding Little League baseball coach. All four of her boys were active on teams. By the time Sherri was in kindergarten, she wanted to do everything her brothers did. When Sherri was in the second grade, Mattie founded a hockey team for children, five of whom were her own. Until she graduated from high school, Sherri was usually the only female on ice. However, she competed every year. When the team would play out of the area, the other teams were surprised and amazed to witness Sherri's exceptional skill.

There are many articles written about numerous subjects, such as sports, music, dance, painting, racing, theater, movies, writing, etc. Write your own article, using the "Five and One" strategy.

Choose a subject. _____

Name _____

Select a famous star, hero, or expert who excels in the subject you have chosen.
Examples: a star, Madonna; an expert, Bill Gates; a heroine, Mother Teresa
Answer the following questions, using the "Five and One" investigative method.

1. Who is the star, hero, or expert you have chosen? _____

_____

_____

2. What is he or she doing? _____

_____

_____

3. When did he or she begin to do the activity that made him or her famous? You can add
   any other detail. _____

_____

_____

4. Where was he or she born? Where does your person perform his or her activity? Where
   did he or she learn to be outstanding? _____

_____

_____

5. Why is this person different or outstanding? Why does your person like the activity?
   Why do you admire your person?_____

_____

_____

6. How did your person become famous? How does your person rank among others?

_____

_____

_____

_____

After you have answered these questions, write the article about your person. Begin your
article with a sentence that will make your readers want to finish reading it.

_____

_____

YOUR MIND'S EYE

Choose the sport from either winter or summer that you know best; then create an athlete in your mind that is playing this sport. Write a sentence that includes a name you give to your athlete, what sport he or she is playing, and where the sport takes place.

_____

What special clothing, shoes, head gear, or gloves is your athlete wearing? What particular equipment is required for this sport?

_____

_____

Is this sport done inside or outside? What does the environment surrounding the event look like? Are there spectators, bleachers, or water? List many details.

_____

_____

_____

On the back of this sheet, draw your athlete in the action of the sport.

Imagine that you are a spectator watching your athlete compete. On notebook paper, describe the entire scene you have invented in your mind. Write about the place and about your athlete's physical description and actions. Study your lists and drawing to get ideas for descriptive action words and other details that you can explain in your paragraph.

Things to Keep in Your Journal

A journal is also called a *diary* or a *log*. Some people keep one for every day of their lives, while others use them to record special events like vacations or projects. However, keeping a journal for any length of time can be more useful than simply recording what you ate for breakfast and dinner. It can serve as a place to brainstorm ideas, to analyze problems, and to remember. A journal can also serve as source material, a place to look when you need ideas for expository writing.

Write about the following two suggestions.

1. Think of something today that might have puzzled you or hurt your feelings. Write a paragraph to describe the scene with details of what you remember seeing, hearing, and feeling. Include conversations. Reread the scene as though you were someone else. Write another paragraph as though you were the other person. Try to explain why the event is confusing or hurtful.

2. Draw a circle on another sheet of paper. Inside the circle, write the name of a subject that is giving you trouble. Draw lines from the circle and write on these lines the various reasons that contribute to your trouble with this subject. Below the circle, list ways you can eliminate the problems.

In three days, read your journal entry again to see whether or not you are managing to deal with your problem more effectively.

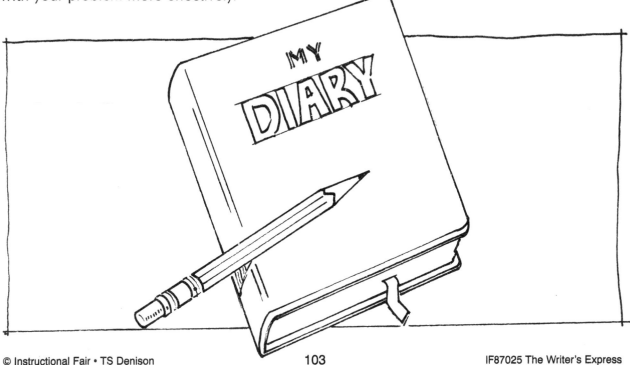

Name _____

WHAT IS FUN AND WHAT IS NOT!

"I hate to do that!" Have you ever said those words? Do you know why you dislike a certain activity? Have you ever said? "I just love this!" What makes you like to do something? Have you ever analyzed exactly what is fun for you to do?

• List one activity you dislike in (A) and one activity you enjoy in (B).

(A) _____   (B) _____

For example: cleaning rabbit's cage   *For example: reading*

• List three reasons you dislike (A).   List three reasons you enjoy (B).
  Examples: It takes too long.   *I learn new ideas.*
  It stinks.   *It is stimulating.*
  It is boring.   *It is peaceful.*

(A) _____   (B) _____

    _____   _____

    _____   _____

• Analyze and compare your lists. Can you determine a type of activity that brings you pleasure?

_____

For example: I like to do things indoors.

Determine the type of activity that you dislike. _____

_____

For example: I don't like to take care of animals.

- What type of activity do you enjoy? Explain in detail why this type of activity makes you happy.

_____

_____

_____

_____

_____

- What type of activity do you dislike? Explain in detail why this type of activity makes you unhappy.

_____

_____

_____

_____

_____

Have you discovered something about your personality? What does this discovery tell you?

_____

_____

_____

_____

_____

_____

_____

_____

_____

_____

_____

_____

_____

_____

Name _____

Do You Measure Up?

Writing an evaluation of how you are doing in a subject in school can be very helpful. You can determine how well you are doing. You can also see where you need to improve.

Choose one of your subjects in school, one that you would like to evaluate.

Subject: _____

What must you do to make good grades in this subject? _____

_____

_____

Which of the activities in regard to this subject are easy for you? _____
Why? _____

_____

_____

Which of the activities in regard to this subject are difficult for you? _____
Why? _____

_____

_____

Write a paragraph in which you explain how you can improve in this subject.

Example: I can improve my grades in math by doing my homework more carefully. I do not always double-check my figures. When I take a test, I am under stress, so I make even more careless mistakes. The proper practice with homework will help me do the right steps on tests and remind me to double-check my figures.

_____

_____

_____

_____

_____

_____

Name _____

WHAT'S IN A NAME?

Your name records you as an individual but may or may not show your heritage, tradition, or the culture of your ancestors. You can explore your name by analyzing in detail what you know about it.

Write your full name on the line below.

_____

first   middle   last   nickname

What do you know about each part of your name?

1. Were you named after a certain person? _____

   _____

2. What do you know about this person? _____

   _____

3. What do you know about the meaning of your name? _____

   _____

4. Which of your names do you like best and least? Why? _____

   _____

5. How did you get your nickname? _____

Write a paragraph explaining how you feel about your name and what it means to you.

Example: I am proud to be named after my Uncle Lennie. He was a hero in France during World War II. We both have nicknames, but they are different so that the family can keep us separated in conversation. The family calls me Len. I plan to do something heroic for my country when I grow up too, like being the first geologist to land on Mars.

_____

_____

_____

_____

_____

_____

Exploring Connections and Contrasts

Some words can be arranged in two types of categories: antonyms and synonyms. Using the words that fall in both categories, you can write a comparison or contrast between you and another person.

Antonyms are words of opposite meanings: sharp/dull; empty/full.

Synonyms are words of similar meanings: couch/sofa; wash/bathe; border/edge.

Think of a friend who is like an antonym to you. This person is opposite to you in some important way. Write the word that best shows how you are opposite this person.

You	Your Person
_____	_____
For example: careful	*thoughtless*

Write one or two sentences that show why you chose these words to describe you and the person you chose.

For example: I am very careful to always remember birthdays of my friends. My friend, Anne, is thoughtless about remembering mine.

_____

_____

_____

_____

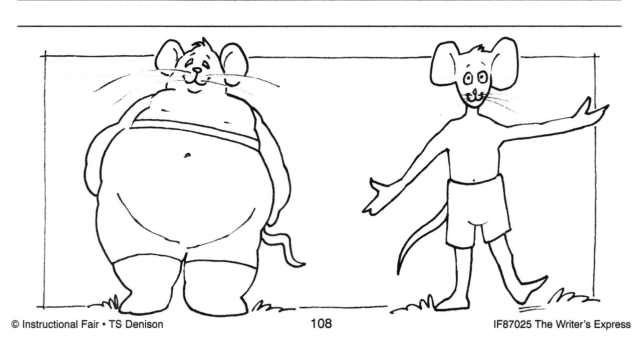

Select another friend who resembles you in more than one way. This person is like a synonym to you. Though he or she may not look like you or even enjoy doing the same activities, the two of you are somehow similar.

Write a word describing you and then write a synonym to describe this second person. Remember these two words should have similar meanings and describe some important detail about you and your second person.

You   Your Second Person

_____   _____

For example: cheerful   *happy*

Write a sentence that includes and explains the synonym you chose for yourself. Write a second sentence that includes and explains the synonym you chose for your second person.

For example: I am a happy person who goes through life looking on the bright side of everything. My friend, Cindy, is always cheerful; she finds a way to make everyone feel better.

_____

_____

Write a paragraph that explains how you and only one of the persons you described are alike OR different. End the paragraph by explaining why you think you and your friend compare or contrast.

_____

_____

_____

_____

_____

_____

_____

_____

_____

_____

WISHING WORDS

Most of us have a desire to excel in some skill that we do not have. This feeling is quite normal. Each of us has special abilities that others do not have. In the left-hand column, list three things you do well. In the right-hand column, list three things you wish you could do well.

Things I Do Well   Things I Wish I Did Well

_____   _____

_____   _____

_____   _____

Choose one of the three skills that you do well. Think of a friend who does not perform this skill as well as you do. Write a note to you from this friend in which he or she describes your ability at performing this skill. Use your friend's way of expressing himself or herself so that the note seems as though it really comes from your friend.

_____

_____

_____

Choose an idea from the right-hand list. Think of a friend who can easily do this activity. Write a note to this friend from you. Write the words as though you were speaking to your friend. Perhaps you want to tell your friend what makes you admire his or her ability. Perhaps you want to say why you wish you had the same ability that your friend does.

Compare the two notes you have written. Send the note you wrote about your friend to him or her.

MAY I INTRODUCE MYSELF?

If you had only a short time to let someone know what makes you an interesting and unique person, what would you say? You would probably want to communicate the most important information about yourself.

To help you get started thinking about your unique qualities, answer the following questions.

1. What is your name? _____

2. What do you like to be called? _____

3. Where do you live? _____

4. What school do you attend, and what grade are you in? _____

5. What is your best subject? _____

6. What are your favorite hobbies? Why? _____
    _____

7. What are you very good at doing? Why? _____
    _____

8. How many brothers and sisters do you have? _____

9. How do you show that you are a good friend to others? _____
    _____

10. What are your dreams for your future? _____
    _____
    _____

11. What makes your family different from others? _____

_____

_____

12. What are you grateful for in life? _____

_____

_____

Now that you have thought about yourself, choose only one idea about yourself that makes you unique or interesting. Write it below.

Analyze the one idea you selected. Make certain you describe your unique quality by using the five Ws: Who? What? When? Where? and Why?

_____

_____

_____

_____

_____

_____

_____

Rewrite your explanation into a finished paragraph. Begin with the most important explanations. Add, delete, and rearrange your words. When you have finished editing, you will have created a short introduction of yourself.

_____

_____

_____

_____

_____

_____

_____

_____

_____

_____

VIDEO GAME FEVER

Kent woke up early on a cold, rainy morning. Something was different. The familiar hum of the electrical appliances was silent. The comforting glow from the night light was out, even the clock numbers were blank. "Oh, no the electricity has gone out," he thought to himself. No fried eggs and bacon, no warm heater in the bathroom, no television—worse— no video games! He slumped back into the bed and tried to ignore the cold sweat coming up on his face as he realized that it was going to be a cold, rainy day without anything special to do.

Wait a minute . . . there is a solution. Why not create your own video game? It can be played however you want it. It can have characters or not. Your invented game could be about any sport or game you can create. Include step-by-step procedures which will tell your readers exactly how to play your new game. You should avoid copying one you already know!

Explain your video game here.

_____

_____

_____

_____

_____

_____

When you have finished, share your ideas with others. You may be on your way to becoming the next video game giant!

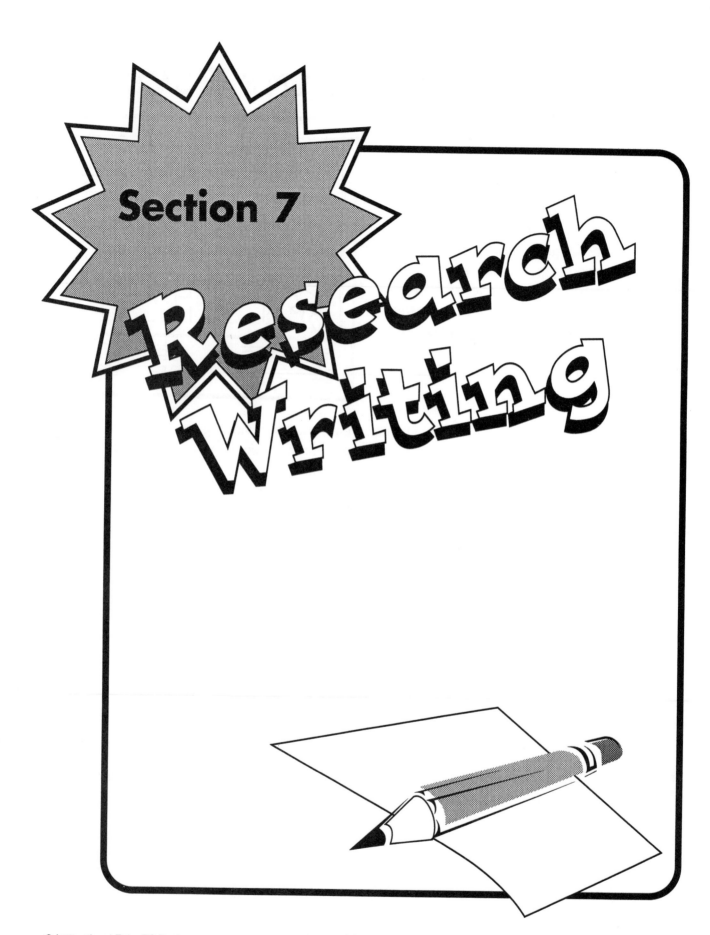

Section 7

Research Writing

LITTLE-KNOWN FACTS

There are so many different varieties of animals that it would be hard for one person to know them all. Each creature on earth fulfills a link in the continuation of life. Every animal has specialized attributes that enable it to survive. The camel has a cavity to carry more water so it can survive in the desert. The owl has soft feathers so it cannot be heard as it flies through the night forest looking for its prey. The beaver's teeth grow throughout its life so it can gnaw on trees and not wear down its teeth.

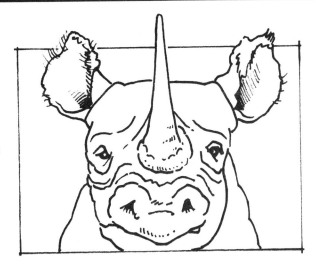

What other little-known facts about animal survival do you know? What obscure facts can you learn by using the Internet and other reference sources? Select three different animals. Research little-known facts about their survival. Find out how they contribute to sustaining life on earth. Write at least three little-known facts for each animal. Make certain you use your own words as you use your resources to find this information.

Animal One _____

_____

_____

_____

Animal Two _____

_____

_____

_____

Animal Three _____

_____

_____

_____

INVESTIGATING AN ENDANGERED SPECIES ON THE INTERNET

What do the rhinoceros, whooping crane, zebra, kimodo dragon, bald eagle, hawksbill turtle, giant panda, giraffe, humpback whale, and hyacinth macaw have in common? They are all part of a long list of endangered species.

Using a computer, look up *endangered species* first in the computer's dictionary and then in its encyclopedia. After you have read the information, answer the questions below in your own words.

What are endangered species? _____

_____

What has made them endangered? _____

_____

_____

Return to the computer.

Click on the Internet. Go to the World Wide Web. On the Web channels, you may select a number of sources for researching *endangered species*. You can click on Research and type in *endangered species*, or you can click on Reference Source. You may choose The Discovery Channel or departments, such as Science. Perhaps you want to begin by taking a shortcut by typing in *endangered species*. Browse and read about endangered species for about ten minutes.

From your research on the computer, select one species that you find most interesting. Write its name, where it is located, and whether it is animal, reptile, fish, insect, bird, etc.

_____

_____

Now that you have selected a specific endangered species, return to the computer again and type in the name of your endangered species. As you search, write the answers to the questions below when you find the information. Write the answers in your *own* words.

Describe your species in detail. _____

_____

_____

What does it need to have to survive, such as food or environment? _____

_____

_____

_____

How have human activities endangered its survival? _____

_____

_____

_____

What could specifically be done to make it safe again? _____

_____

_____

_____

What makes this species unique? _____

_____

_____

Write about this species in your *own* words. Use description and details to give complete information about your species: its habitat, how it is endangered, why it is unique, and ways in which it could be made safe again. Include your personal opinions along with the factual data you accumulated from your Internet research.

_____

_____

_____

_____

_____

_____

_____

_____

Your Hometown Climate, "Weather" You Like It or Not

Whether you meet a friend or stranger, a likely first comment is about the weather. It is only natural. The activity of the atmosphere affects us daily, whether the weather is hot and sunny or cold and rainy.

Weather is the changing state of temperature, humidity, air pressure, precipitation, and wind of any area. However, *climate* is the normal or predictable atmospheric conditions of weather over a longer period of time, such as arid, temperate, tropical, or polar.

Describe the climate where you live. Consider the seasons of the year and how the weather changes in each season to create your climate. Include temperature ranges, types of precipitation, and wind. All these factors make your climate normal and predictable.

_____

_____

_____

_____

Find a detailed map and locate your hometown. Consider the geographical location, nearby bodies of water, elevation, mountains, and valleys.

Select three facts about the geographical location and the surrounding environment.

On the back of this sheet, write your facts and how you think they affect the climate.

Look your area up in the encyclopedia. Determine whether your ideas were correct.

WHAT IF IT DID NOT HAPPEN THAT WAY?

In the course of historical events, it has frequently happened that major outcomes were greatly influenced by a minor incident. Some people call such an occurrence *luck* or *fate*.

Details can change outcomes. For example, in 42 B.C., if the Roman Emperor Julius Caesar had stayed away from the forum on March 15, Brutus might have lost courage to stab him to death. If the bacteriologist, Alexander Fleming, had not taken notice of the strange reaction of the bits of fungus he was about to throw away, penicillin would not have been discovered as early as 1922.

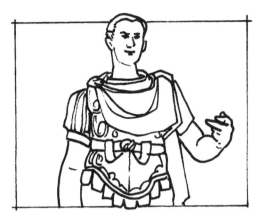

1. Using resource books, look up a historical event. As you read about the event, study the details of minor incidents that determined the final outcome of the event.

2. Select one of the minor incidents you found and write it in your notebook.

3. Describe what the final outcome of the event might have been like if this minor incident had not happened at all. Next, describe what might have happened if the minor incident had been slightly or greatly altered.

4. When you are satisfied with your analysis, you are ready to write an analytical essay about the importance of the minor incident to the event.
   A. Write a general description of the event. Describe when and where the event happened. Be certain to write it in your own words. Do not copy from the resource.
   B. Describe the importance of the minor incident to your event. Describe when and where the minor incident happened during the event.
   C. Explain how the minor incident affected the final outcome of the event.
   D. Describe either how you think the minor incident might have been altered or how it might not have occurred at all.
   E. Close your essay with your analysis of what the outcome of the event would have been if the minor incident had either not happened at all or had been altered.

RESEARCH AND REWRITE
IT IN YOUR OWN WORDS

When you write a report, research sources are necessary to investigate the subject. In writing a report, you are required to rewrite the research in your own words. This writing method is called *paraphrasing*.

Read the following information about Native American Indians.

Two hundred years ago, there were multitudes of vastly different tribes living in the forests, mountains, deserts, and large water regions throughout North America. Each tribe had its own culture, language, and customs. They hunted, farmed, lived in communities, and worshiped. They enjoyed many old rituals such as weddings and festivals. They mourned for their dead and celebrated their living.

When the settlers came from Europe, they gradually grew to be in conflict with the Native-American culture. Europeans mistakenly decided that the Native Americans they called Indians were savage and ignorant. The Native Americans lived a simpler life than the invaders and did not have the European forms of government, language, and modern technology. Also, the new Americans had more powerful tools and weapons. The settlers cleared the land to make room for towns, roads, and shops, eventually wiping out a centuries-old culture by force and devastation. The Native Americans' style of living disappeared. By 1830 most Native Americans had been consigned by their conquerors to live on parcels of land called reservations. The way of life of the free and independent Native American was altered forever.

Using this research information on Native Americans, paraphrase one portion of the above paragraphs. Be certain to keep the facts correct, but use your own words to express the main ideas.

_____

_____

_____

_____

_____

SELECTING THE BEST

Before reporters begin writing about a subject, they conduct research. From their research, they gain information. Reporters usually acquire more information than necessary to write their articles. In this way, they are able to select only the best information for their articles.

For example, if a reporter wanted to write about a skier and the 1998 Winter Olympics, the reporter would first observe the skier, the sport, and the Olympic Games. The following are the reporter's notes after observing a skier at the Olympics.

Reporter's Notes:
red, white, and blue with 10 on the back/bent over like a bull ready to charge/legs wide on shining skies/ready to zip downhill/into the belly of the valley/on the mountaintop lifting fog, sun, so bright, need sunglasses

Reporter's Research:
Nagano County, Japan/1998 Olympics/February/new hotels, roads small and winding around the mountains/traffic-laden/fog on the hills/steep/hot springs, bridge with new statues on its posts of a skier and a snowboarder/3,000 athletes, coaches, and officials come from 83 countries/dreams of gold/new bullet train line built especially for this event, the Asma No. 500 to rocket 630 passengers from Tokyo to Nagano/Nagano 700 years old/keystone of city is Zenkoji Temple, 400-year-old bell rung for opening Olympic ceremonies February 7.

Read the sample from the reporter's article about the skier. Notice which details the reporter used from the notes and the research. What kind of information did the reporter use at the beginning of the article? The details at the end of the article are less important ideas. Notice the information that the reporter selected for the article.

Reporter's Article

On this February 8, high above the new hotels of Nagano, I watched a youth with a dream of gold. She appeared anxious to add her signature to the smooth, white back of the mountains. The American skier focused all her concentration on the icy strip in front of her. Through sunglasses, millions of excited eyes were positioned, on a shining moment, on her, only one of the 3,000 athletes, coaches, and officials who came from 83 countries of the world. The skier prepared to zip into the valley below. We held our breath as she pushed off.

Using the reporter's notes and research, write a reporter's article about this skier at the 1998 Winter Olympics. Begin your article with the Five Ws: Who, What, When, Where, and Why. After you write the important information at the beginning of the article, follow it with less important details. Select only the best details for your article.

_____

_____

_____

_____

_____

_____

_____

_____

_____

_____

_____

_____

_____

_____